Copyright @ 2024 by Maria L. Casas

All rights reserved. No part of this publication may be reproduced, distributed, or transmitted in any form or by any means, including photocopying, recording, or other electronic or mechanical methods, without the prior written permission of the publisher, except in the case of brief quotations embodied in critical reviews and certain other noncommercial uses permitted by copyright law. For permission requests, write to the publisher at the address below.

Dr. Maria L. Casas
Email: purifiedministries@yahoo.com

Church mailing Address:
Remnant Church WestCo
2088S. Atlantic Blvd suite # 261
Monterey Park CA. 91754

Social Media:
Maria Casas - on Facebook
mariacasasq - on Instagram

THE HOLY BIBLE, NEW INTERNATIONAL VERSION®, NIV® Copyright © 1973, 1978, 1984, 2011 by Biblica, Inc.® Used by permission. All rights reserved worldwide.

KJV Public Domain

Scripture taken from the New King James Version®. Copyright © 1982 by Thomas Nelson. Used by permission. All rights reserved.

Darby Translation Public Domain

The Holy Bible, English Standard Version (ESV) is adapted from the Revised Standard Version of the Bible, copyright Division of Christian Education of the National Council of the Churches of Christ in the U.S.A. All rights reserved.

Holy Bible, New Living Translation, copyright © 1996, 2004, 2015 by Tyndale House Foundation. Used by permission of Tyndale House Publishers, Inc., Carol Stream, Illinois 60188. All rights reserved.

A Beautiful Exchange
Table of Contents

Acknowledgements   2

Forward by Dr. Roseanna Roman   3

1. Did I Ever Stand a Chance?... 4
2. Organized Evil.. 12
3. Carefree.. 16
4. Intimidation.. 26
5. Success is Spelled R-I-S-K... 30
6. We are Body, Soul, and Spirit... 36
7. Our Little Family Moved to the Center of Town........................ 43
8. Everything Changes... 56
9. Time to Immigrate to the United States.................................... 66
10. The Dog Was Vicious... 76
11. Cesar Chavez and the UFW... 83
12. My First BFF... 87
13. Mom Steps in and Saves the Day.. 96
14. Culture Shock…Again.. 101
15. Your Blouse is Inappropriate.. 110
16. My First Real Date.. 117
17. He Tried to Kidnap Me.. 124
18. If Tomorrow Starts Without Me.. 132
19. The Near Death Experience (NDE).. 137
20. She Made It Through! She is Awake!...................................... 145
21. Back in School.. 153
22. Did You Hear That the Overdose Made Her Crazy?................ 159
23. The Depth of My Bondage... 169
24. Threatened With a Knife.. 178
25. You Can't Go Home Again... 191
26. You Are Pregnant... 204
27. My Appointment ~ A Beautiful Exchange............................... 215
28. Mom, I Have Been Saved!... 222
29. My Little Red New Testament Revealed................................. 228

What Others Are Saying... 236

Acknowledgements

I want to thank my amazing husband, Pastor Clemente Casas my partner in life for forty-three years who faithfully stands by me. He has been my constant encouragement in writing this book believing that my story would truly help others find hope.

Shout out to my kids and grandkids for not laughing at me when I told them I'd be writing this book. Lol/jk.

I also appreciate and acknowledge my precious Mom, Dad, my grandparents and my siblings who are all part of my life story.

Thank you Jody Day for your valuable time, energy and work in editing and bringing this book to print.

And of course, I want to thank my Lord, Savior and best friend, Jesus Christ, without whom I would have no redemptive story to tell.

FORWARD

"A Beautiful Exchange"

In writing this book Dr. Maria Casas was willing to dive into both pleasant and painful realities that make up her journey. I believe the reader will find, hope and inspiration that will lead to Truth.
With honesty and transparency, she communicates poignant incidences of victimization that should have destroyed her life. But also beautiful victories that seem to be nothing less than miracles.

Whether you are a teenager or an adult, many will relate to her experiences as I found myself relating to the accounts in these pages. She takes you on a journey that will hold your interest and will leave you deep in thought long after you close the pages.

The Woman of God she is today is a direct result of her life experiences, but also her surrender and commitment to The God who saw it all.

She inspires you to stop running from your healing, run towards God, and embrace the wholeness and wellness he offers. He will never reject those who come to him. Jeremiah 17

Apostle, Dr. Roseanna Roman
Vice-Pres. Of Evangelism HSBN.tv
Co-Founder of CWWN.tv

A Beautiful Exchange
by Maria Casas

My Sorrow for His Joy

"You saw me before I was born. Every day of my life was recorded in your book. Every moment was laid out before a single day had passed." NIV Psalm 139: 16

Chapter 1
Did I Ever Stand a Chance?

Mom always made doing laundry a group chore; the clothes had to be folded just so, and she checked. We were well organized, and everyone had a part to play. "Tight and neat" was her motto; we didn't even need to iron afterward. One particular Sunday late afternoon, I was putting my portion of the laundry away; I held the folded pile close to my nose and inhaled deeply. I loved the scent of laundry softener. It reminded me of a new start, a fresh beginning. Sometimes, that's what you crave: a new start, a "do-over." The ring of our house phone brought my mind back to the task at hand. "It's for you!" my sister called out. Placing my basket on the floor, I went to answer.

"Hey, You busy?" I heard my friend's familiar voice ask. "Just finishing up the laundry."

"Can I come over? I need a trim on my feathered wings." Farah Faucet hair was all the rage. All of our friends had feathered bangs.

"Sure come over, I can do it." Her house was just down the street, so it wasn't long before she was at my door. "Come on in."

We walked to my room, chatting about all the latest things happening in our fifteen-year-old lives. Someone was constantly breaking up or fighting. There was always a party somewhere, and plans had to be made.

Suddenly, the house phone rang out again. "Get the phone!" everyone shouted in unison from different rooms. I was the closest, so I picked up the receiver. "Hell-O," I said playfully. It was my eighteen-year-old boyfriend on the other end, and he sounded angry. Someone had told him that I had done something that he didn't like, and he was calling me demanding answers. I denied doing it, but his anger was not going away that easily. He continued criticizing, talking down to me, and angrily belittling me. We went back and forth.

I had begun to recognize a pattern of abuse and had seen this done to my friends regularly by their boyfriends. I hurt for them when I saw how their boyfriends humiliated them in front of others. I wondered why they allowed it, why they subjected themselves to this. Although I was very much in love with this abusive young man, he didn't have the same love for me. I felt the familiar knot in my stomach, and it was dawning on me where this relationship was going.

He continued arguing his point. Frustrated, I said, "So what do you want? You want to break up?"

"I'm not saying that." He snapped back.

"He sees this constant arguing as normal," I thought. He wants a girlfriend to mistreat and abuse. For some reason, this was seen as cool in the circles he ran in. They all did it. Even the girlfriends saw jealousy and control as a sign of how much their boyfriends loved them.

I would not allow it, " I don't think this is working out!" I broke up with him and hung up the phone.

It was common to hear of friends being bullied, cussed at, and even beaten by their boyfriends. Most went on to get pregnant and have babies from these abusive boyfriends, and I had determined that this would not be me. "I promised myself, "I will not allow anyone to treat me that way. I won't allow them to break me."

Devastated, I returned to my room; this was my first love. Feeling crushed, I sighed, blinking rapidly, refusing to allow the tears to flow. I told myself, " I will not cry. I refused to allow myself to fall apart," but I was losing the battle. All I had ever wanted was to belong, be truly loved by someone, and find true community.

I put on a fake smile as I walked into the bedroom where my friend sat waiting. "Let's get to it!" I said, pointing to the chair in front of my dresser mirror. She sat; I placed a towel on her shoulders and grabbed the scissors. I began cutting her hair, and she started talking, telling me what she had been up to and the latest gossip, but her voice trailed off. Suddenly, something very peculiar began to occur.

    A thick haze came over me, and I felt as though I was hypnotized. I began to hear a voice, and simultaneously, a strange, soothing feeling enveloped me. It washed over me and inside me, sort of the same way that your first drink of hard liquor goes down inside your belly. It started on top of my head and ran to my feet. It was overwhelming, and it took over me completely!

    A clear voice began to reason with me, "Aren't you tired of how everyone treats you?" I was tired but I wasn't despondent. "Nothing you do ever works out." The voice connected with me in the strongest way possible. It wasn't the content of what was being said as much as that there was a power behind those words. They were bewitching. I didn't even question where this voice was coming from or that it was odd, even scary, to feel how I felt. This thing had me in its complete control. "No one cares about you, not even your family." It continued. "You get blamed for everything." I listened intently, feeling increasingly hypnotized by every word spoken. I could not reason.

    The more the voice spoke, the stronger that soothing came over me. It almost felt like someone was stroking my shoulders with their warm hand in a comforting manner.

    The voice said, " You don't have to put up with this anymore. Why don't you take some pills, sleep, and wake up in heaven." I was instantly and wholly convinced of this suggestion. It was strange. I wasn't emotional, and I was very calm, but the words spoken to me connected to my inner core. I was on autopilot, and every suggestion exuded a strong hypnotic strength that I was powerless to resist.

Strangely enough, I continued cutting my friend's hair and carried on a conversation with her. At the same time, the voice and soothing feeling kept increasing. I vaguely remember the back-and-forth dialogue with her. She sat facing my dresser mirror, and I was behind her, so I caught a glance of myself smiling strangely as I sprayed her hair with water, parted her hair, lifted portions, measured, and cut. My eyes looked glassy, and I looked as if I knew something no one else did.

She was unaware that I had succumbed to this strong, seducing demon. How does this happen with her in the room and a house filled with lively activity in the background?

I was convinced I was going to do as the voice said. Standing there smiling, I felt I had a secret that made me happy. I couldn't wait to finish my friend's haircut and get on with taking the pills.

I finished her cut, combed her bangs back, and raked them with my finger, causing them to feather as they slowly fell to the sides of her face. She looked satisfied. I removed the towel from around her shoulders and vaguely remember walking with her, making plans to go out later that week. I saw her to the door, and we said our goodbyes. I calmly came back to my room and put my hair-cutting tools away. The strange smile never left my face.

The soothing presence never loosened its influencing grip on me. Instead, it seemed to double up its grip, and the voice gave me clear instructions, which I followed precisely. "Go to the kitchen. Get that stool, put it in front of that upper cupboard. Get on the stool, open the upper cupboard door, and go to the top shelf."

The shelf was high over my head; our family considered this our junk cupboard, filled with forgotten objects. Boxes filled with "things." I had no clue what was on the lower shelves, much less the top shelf at the ceiling level. "Get on the stool!" the voice instructed. "Open the cupboard, look in the very back of the very top shelf, get that metal box, open it." The voice now came quicker and began to sound like orders, which I promptly obeyed. "Move those documents at the very edge of the box, get that bottle.".

As I moved the documents, a brand-new yellow prescription bottle of codeine pills became visible. My mom had just filled the prescription because of a surgery she had just had. I didn't know the pills were there, yet I was going directly to them. There was no searching or rifling through everything, but instead, making precise moves that led me straight to the pills.

My family was home, and everyone was busy preparing for the coming week and finishing household chores. No one asked what I was up to. I didn't try to hide it. I was being controlled by an outside entity that was now inside me. I vaguely remember my sister walking through the kitchen; someone else came in to get a glass of water or something. No one seemed to notice that I was under the complete influence of something evil. It had me like a puppet, following instructions and setting up my death.

The voice continued to direct me soothingly, the warm hand stroking my shoulders and back, "Put the box back, close the cupboard, put the stool back in its place, get a glass of water, go in the bathroom, your family will think you are simply taking a shower."

The instructions were coming faster and faster. I held the full bottle of codeine in one hand and the glass in the other. I could hear the sound of commercials in the living room. Someone was watching TV; I believe it was my Dad. I saw the bluish hue of the TV through the hall as I made my way to the restroom to kill myself.

While in the restroom, the soothing increased. The voice directed me, "Fill your glass with water; take all the pills." I did as I was told, "Open the medicine cabinet, see what else is in there." The voice seemed delighted at my compliance. I turned towards the medicine cabinet; I could see my reflection in the mirror, again the glassy eyes, the strange, smug smile.

I found a full box of extra-strength pain relievers in the medicine cabinet. "Take all of them, just to be sure." The voice was energetic and frenzied, filled with excitement. I had no alarm in my soul or concept of reality. I could not discern nor see that this was an evil entity directing me. Maybe this is what a hypnotized zombie looks like, just following directions with no will of my own.

"Take a shower." I may have even been humming in the shower, the warm water running down my hair and face, as I rinsed off the fragrant shampoo. I dried off, neatly replaced the towel on the rack, and dressed for bed.

"Write a goodbye note." The instructions continued. This was a "suicide note," but this entity was shrewdly selective with its words.

Back in my room, I pulled a sheet of paper off my school binder, found a pen, sat on the bed, and obediently began to write. I remember writing, again vaguely, that I was leaving some of my belongings to my sisters. I do remember feeling happy that I could be generous to them. Other than that, I remember nothing else I wrote.

"Lie down, sleep; you will wake up in heaven." There was never any resistance on my part. I obediently laid down, freshly showered, with freshly laundered clothes that smelled of fabric softener.

On the other side of our bedroom were my two younger sisters sleeping. The drugs were taking effect. I now felt heavy and sleepy and was losing the ability to function. There was a long dresser in between our beds. I placed the note and empty pill bottles on the dresser and quickly fell into a deep, deep sleep. I was not supposed ever to wake up again.

Did I ever stand a chance? Was my life that bad that I would be willing to end it?

Chapter 2
Organized Evil

In hindsight, as I consider the destructive path my life eventually took, I am now acutely aware that we are the object of God's love and constant pursuit. However, in light of what I just wrote about my suicide attempt, you may say, "This statement contradicts your reality." Although I didn't understand this then, I believe so now. God's love pursues us, but we do have an enemy, so we also automatically become the focus of Satan's hate. Many don't believe in spiritual evil, but no one can convince me it isn't real. I have confronted it and almost lost my life to it.

Without consent, we become the target of this organized evil, its constant attempt at destroying our lives with shrewd strategy, snuffing them out before birth even, if possible. This evil is relentless.

Thinking of my formative years, it strikes me that I was surrounded by love and hard-working, ethical, religious, decent human beings who were doing their best to provide a good life for me, yet I never stood a chance. Why do I say this?

Because my loving family didn't know that spiritual wickedness had formulated an assignment against me as it does for all humans. It intended to destroy my hope, twist and warp my innocence victimize me and contort my image of The Creator. But the ultimate goal was to destroy me utterly.

How does one survive this reality? What can we do to protect ourselves and our families? What are we dealing with, and can it even be defeated?

Please stick with me as I share my story. I believe it will become clear that, yes, there is hope, there is an answer, and it is entirely accessible to you and anyone else who is willing to receive it.

"The thief comes not, but to steal, and to kill, and to destroy: I am come that they might have life, and that they might have it more abundantly.." KJV John 10:10

A Time of Innocence

No matter where you were born or who your parents were, it didn't happen in secret. Your birth was a celebrated event by heaven. There was great rejoicing, wonder, and anticipation to see what immense significance this tiny little being would bring to the world. There is a flash of light at the moment of conception that baffles scientists to this day. A soul is a valuable and precious thing in the eyes of heaven and the object of God's intense love.

My family lived in a small, beautiful, lush green village surrounded by hills in Mexico. I especially loved it in the rainy season, with rain hitting hard on the tile roofs and making a sound that resembled popcorn popping.

The frequent clouds gave the surrounding scenery a blue tinge as if it had been washed with denim and a fresh scent that can't be described adequately with words. It must be experienced and is something you don't forget.

Sometimes, the rain came down so violently that it sounded angry, but it soon calmed down to a rhythmic, calming pace. It was mesmerizing to watch the runoff off the roof, rushing quickly down the street, making a swishing sound as it cleansed the cobblestones of dirt and debris, leaving them shiny and new.

The strength of the run-off produced new, fast-moving streams here and there where they hadn't been the day before. Colorful flowers soon bloomed everywhere, even where they weren't planted.

Then there was the river with its menacing, turbulent waters churning past the giant beige and grey boulders, becoming impassable.

Storms can create a gloomy atmosphere, but after the rain and downpour, what beauty is left behind!

I see life like that now. There have been terrible, gloomy, dark clouds and even some horrible destructive storms. However, there is beauty that can arise from torment. If anyone had told me this before I met Christ, I would have responded with a blank stare, wondering, "How?" How can this be?

You see, to heal, we must be determined that we will not become stuck, reliving the storms with every detail, and always feeling the painful experience.

But how? How do we become unstuck? I have found that it's not always easy. Okay, it's never easy, but then nothing is. I heard someone say. "Doing the work necessary for healing is hard."

Doing nothing and living in denial is hard. So pick your "hard"."

I have determined to allow God to give me the courage to heal; it is not easy, but neither is remaining broken.

Chapter 3
Carefree

Memories

Our village had no electricity, cars, or indoor plumbing. To get to the village, one exited the bus up on the paved highway. Then we walked downhill for about 45 minutes through cornfields, stone boundary fences, small streams, and wilderness. Eventually, you'd find yourself confronted by the river, which one crossed on a flimsy rope bridge suspended from a giant tree, used mainly in the rainy season to get to the village. In the dry season, the river could be safely crossed, jumping from stone to stone. If you had a horse or donkey, well, then you had it made.

The village was isolated, and its citizens knew little of the outside world. I remember my grandmother telling me that once she knelt in fear because she heard a strange sound in the sky and then saw a small plane over the village. It made her think that the world was ending. We giggled when she told us this story, but she was genuinely scared. Many years later, we would fly her to the US in a 747; she became a pro and a fearless flyer.

There were no phones in the village, but somehow, when you were dropped off at the top of the hill, everyone knew you were coming.

Our first home was nicknamed "The White House" because it was whitewashed, highly visible, isolated, and alone on the hillside. I was the second child born to my parents. It was a home birth, so when family members speak of my older sibling Vincent and my birth, they say, "You were born up on the hill, in the white house." How many people can claim that? I suppose this should have been a clue that the "US of A" would be our home one day.

The first years of my life were spent there. I vividly remember a toddler bouncing up and down mischievously on the hard bed. With every bounce, a baby lying on the same bed bounced and scooted until it finally rolled head-first between the wall and the bed. I recall mom rushing to pull the baby out, who was screaming, upside down, stuck in the crack between the bed and the wall. Mom quickly grabbed the baby and scolded the toddler while bouncing and hushing the screaming infant.

Mom says this memory is impossible because I was that baby, and the toddler was my brother Vince. I tell her I do remember. That room was sunny. Looking up while lying on that hard bed, I saw a square wooden cradle with a wire mesh bottom. It was suspended from the ceiling by ropes. She says that the memory is correct. This was a family crib our grandfather had made. It was passed around to whoever needed it in the family. She was, however, surprised that I had such an early memory.

What memories come to mind when you think of your life?

Years back, as I studied "healing from severe trauma," I heard a teacher mention that deep trauma causes us to have memory gaps. Seasons, or entire years, that we may only have fuzzy memories of or no memories of at all. This can likely mean that these year gaps are not remembered because the trauma was inflicted upon us during those years. He said, "Our survival instinct kicks in and subconsciously erases that memory."

Another memory I have as a toddler is of my brother Vince and I in a field of very tall grass, running so fast that it seemed our feet would outrun our little bodies. The blurry, full-grown grass passed by and hit my face and arms as we picked up speed, my brother holding my hand, wind in our faces, as we stomped through wildflowers, then suddenly stopped!

Our hearts were pounding, our feet on the edge and just short of an old, deep well with no surrounding wall. A sudden, unspoken wave of fear hit us both, our breath coming in gasps. We took a quick peripheral glance at one another and realized we had stopped just in time, so no harm was done. Shaking it off without a word. I felt a tug as my brother pulled me quickly in a different direction, and off we ran just as fast as before. Laughing that joyful, squealing laugh that only little children experience. We never spoke of this dangerous event again. It happened, and now it was behind us.

"Carefree". Do you remember being carefree? No matter how traumatic the event, do you remember being able to shake it off and quickly change directions?

Many of us live with resentment because of some neglect or abuse we were subjected to by a significant, meaningful person in our lives. It may be a parent or family member, a boss, a Pastor, or a loved, trusted friend.

We live with a recording that automatically turns on, begins to repeat, and proceeds to rehearse blow-by-blow the painful events inflicted upon us. The memory is fresh even many years later. Unconsciously, we dwell on the thoughts, connect strongly to and wallow in the emotions. We nurture the pain, the regret, the bitterness, and the trauma.

It is exhausting and time-consuming, distracting from today's beauty. We invest resources, time, and energy into this ritual that has become a part of our person. We shortchange loved ones who are trying to do life with us.

Unknowingly, we create an atmosphere that works as an incubator to keep this brokenness alive within us. We are also teaching those around us something; we are teaching them how to be broken.

Once a day, at least, we bring out some aspect of the trauma. Because, of course, we have triggers. Smells, voices, mustaches, specific phrases, and sounds. When triggered, the memory emerges in full color, HD, and 3D, and we find ourselves plunged into the "feel-a-vision" experience.

Every hurtful, painful memory comes in sharp, still fresh. Some are even stronger than when we had the original experience. It happens automatically. Most of the time, we don't even realize when it started; we naturally flow into these thoughts. They become a ritual, a familiar part of our identity.

We were created with a strong survival instinct meant to be triggered when in danger. But trauma has it malfunctioning, and now we have no off button. As a result, like a computer program, it now runs consistently in the background, depleting our energy.

Our triggers call us to action. We create new walls. We check and refortify old walls, and we develop roadblocks for self-protection. Not realizing we are walling ourselves in as we attempt to wall the dangerous people out.

As a consequence, we become very limited and closed off, never reaching our full potential. We lose the ability to shake things off, to change directions. We begin to lose our vibrant color, becoming muted and diluted. We lose our full strength and zeal for life. We lose our enjoyment of the simple things. After too many years in this condition, our life eventually goes grey. Many will look for some substance to relieve the pain and thus become dependent and addicted to this substance.

Ironically, we usually wall ourselves off from healthy relationships that mean well. Yet toxic predators know how to get us to open the gate willingly.

"Finally, brethren, whatsoever things are true, whatsoever things are honest, whatsoever things are just, whatsoever things are pure, whatsoever things are lovely, whatsoever things are of good report; if there be any virtue, and if there be any praise, think on these things." Philippians 4:8 KJV

Living with Unhealed Trauma

Dad, like most men in the village, had long work days away from home. As a small child, I don't remember him being around much. I do remember Mom and her seemingly never-ending chores.

In my eyes, Mom seemed like a juvenile forced to put on big people clothes. Shoes that were much too big for her. Forced to take responsibility for a large, "real" home and then "real" children. I felt like she mustered up the courage and just did it! She somehow ran the household and found time to love and nurture us. She was creative, fun, and playful with my brother and me. But when Dad returned home from work, something curious would happen. She instantly became nervous and clumsy. I don't have a particular memory, just a sense that the atmosphere would change. Her feelings of intimidation and maybe even fear were palpable, even to a small child. The amazing thing is that somehow, despite her trauma, Mom was still able to provide a healthy home for us.

That's not always the case. Trauma causes us to lose our confidence, and we can't seem to begin to do those things that we once did easily. We begin to diminish in our own eyes.

We don't realize that those who neglected us, failed to nurture and protect us and seemed distant, uncaring and abusive also have a story. They may have also experienced trauma, neglect, abuse, harsh words, betrayal, abandonment, and painful treatment. Something definitely happened to them that handicapped their ability to nurture us.

They were once young and had dreams, and their life was once colorful and carefree. Most likely they did the best they could with the baggage they had to carry in their own life.

If life broke them, well, then they were good to no one. Sadly, not even themselves. They existed in survival mode. Most had no answers to life's destructive patterns either and spent their lives building walls of protection for themselves.

We waste many years regretting the legacy handed to us, what "they" did to us, and how "they" denied us love and attention. Why weren't "they" there for us? Are we that worthless?

But if we are going to get unstuck, we must realize that that season is over, be willing to peel back the layers and allow God to do the work. Let God tell you your worth.

How do you price a work of art?

I heard from an antique art dealer that, first, the object's rarity is considered, and then second, how much is someone willing to pay for it?

Well, you are one of a kind—the only one with your exact DNA. You are unique and wonderfully made, and as far as worth, well, Jesus paid for you with his precious blood. The highest price that could ever be paid for you. You are invaluable.

"knowing that you were not redeemed with corruptible things, like silver or gold, from your aimless conduct received by tradition from your fathers. 19 but with the precious blood of Christ, a lamb without blemish or spot…" 1 Peter 1:18-19 NKJ

I once had a conversation with an inmate in a prison. She sat across a table from me; sadness had left permanent lines on her face that betrayed her attempt at acting "happy." She was doing hard time. Unsolicited, she began to talk to me about very painful memories. She spoke of what her mother did and didn't do for her. Her face grimaced with pain. Her eyes filled with tears that rolled down her cheeks, forming a trail that flowed consistently throughout the telling of her story.

I felt her deep pain and prayed silently, "Jesus, what would you tell her if you were sitting here?". I spoke carefully, sensing His presence in our midst.

"How old are you?" I asked.

"I'm 67."

"Do you have children or grandchildren?"

"Yes, I do."

"Were you a good Mother to your children?"

Her tears stopped, and she looked at me with a puzzled look. She did not answer verbally; she simply looked down and slowly shook her head.

"Were you a good Grandmother to your Grand-babies?" Again, she shook her head, beginning to get the message.

"Oh, my dear sister, you were handed a terrible legacy. I'm sorry that your Mom did not cherish you. Your heavenly Father cherishes you, though; it's time for you to change that legacy." I said softly. Sensing the precious presence of God increase in our midst, I continued, "You have allowed your pain, resentment, and bitterness to steal your younger years. Let Jesus heal you. Change your lineage, and give your kids and grandkids something redeeming and beautiful to remember you by."

Her eyes were filled with tears, but now she nodded in agreement.

"You may have a lifetime of falling. They may have learned how to fail from watching your life. Now teach them how to GET UP!"

She looked at me, and it seemed like her light turned on, the "aha moment" people talk about.   Maybe you didn't do so well at the beginning or the middle, but it's important how you finish. Finish well, and change your lineage.

God redeems wasted time!

The devil has us wasting years in regret, hurt, and crippling resentment. So much so that it has prevented us from creating the healthy, beautiful legacy that we should hand down to our kids and grandkids; it's their season now. We are supposed to be handing them a healthy legacy. It's time to take the focus off of ourselves.

We can't hand them a legacy of pain, a legacy of bitterness and brokenness. Turn to Jesus in surrender, focus, do the hard work of healing, and stop the cycle.

"So I will restore to you the years that the swarming locust has eaten, The crawling locust, The consuming locust, And the chewing locust, My great army which I sent among you.

26You shall eat in plenty and be satisfied, And praise the name of the Lord your God, Who has dealt wondrously with you; And My people shall never be put to shame." Joel 2: 25 - 26 ESV

Chapter 4
Intimidation

You may be a competent individual and possess specific abilities and talents. You may naturally and easily flow in your skills without effort or thought. Yet when fear, intimidation, and insecurity come into your soul, you lose your confidence. You become clumsy when you've been abused, gas lighted, or put in a position of helplessness for an extended period.

Sometimes, it may even seem like "You can't do anything right," especially if this treatment comes from someone you respect. Your mental health suffers, and eventually, even your physical health will decline.

People respond to trauma in different ways. You may shrink and never try anything outside your comfort zone. Or you may become a fighter, determined that no one is going to keep you down. You become a decisive overachiever, a control freak, determined to prove your naysayers wrong accomplishing many things and becoming very successful. Either way, it is unhealthy because both the "shrinker" and the "fighter" come from a place of fear.

This is what I believe happened to Mom. She carried trauma and was heavily intimidated by Dad. He was not menacing; he spoke gently and seemed like a quiet soul around us. He seemed like a different person with her. He talked down on her and criticized her efforts. He demeaned her with cutting words without even raising his voice.

Because of how they started their life together, it set a pattern for how they would relate to one another for the rest of their marriage. They had a painful history together. You see, he had taken her by force from one of the village celebrations. It was a kidnapping. It was a common thing in the villages back then. If a young man saw a girl he wanted, he just took her and kidnapped her.

I heard that the kidnapping occurred as follows.

Mom chatted lightheartedly with a few friends as they walked towards the church square, excitedly carrying baskets filled with traditional, colorful paper banners with which they would be decorating for a coming celebration.

Dad and two others rode by her on their horses, snatched her up, and rode off into the hills. Her hip was permanently injured because of the way she was carried on the horse. One of many painful reminders she was left with from this traumatizing event.

I cannot imagine my Mom's fear. The men carried guns, and she was held against her will. Mom was naive and a very decent girl.

They spent time up in the hills, moving from place to place hiding from those looking for her. Mom had lost a shoe in the process. She wasn't dressed warmly and had to walk on sharp rocks and vegetation for days. Dad made her write a letter to her parents that she had left of her free will.

Mom later became his wife, and after he married her, they rejoined the community in the small village. They set up a household together because that's what you did back then. No counseling, no crime, just shake it off and move on. Her parents believed what was written in the letter to be true. So initially when she ran into her family at a village event, it added insult to injury as her family just looked at her and gave her the cold shoulder. Her dad and brothers wouldn't speak to her for some time.

When her first child, my older brother Vince, was born, he was born weak, malnourished, and nervous because she was weak, malnourished, and nervous during her pregnancy. He didn't really walk until after I did. I was one year and a half younger than he. Even though he could, he didn't speak much. I remember him sitting quietly on the patio floor, his big, beautiful, sad eyes always taking everything in.

Neither I nor my siblings knew how our parents had gotten together until we were grown. I recall being twelve years old and my brother and I hanging out on our front porch with friends, playing with the Ouija board. He and I placed our fingers on the planchette and asked the Ouija board, "What color was our Mom's wedding dress when she married?"

The answer came: She- Did- Not- Wear- a- dress.

Puzzled with this answer, we ran into the house, found Mom in the kitchen, and asked in unison, "Mom, what color was your wedding dress?" Mom scoffed slightly, and she just kept cooking. Without even turning to look at us, said, "I wasn't wearing a dress! I wore someone's old pants."

My brother and I looked at one another, freaked out at the Ouija's accuracy. We didn't even think of asking her why she would wear someone's old pants.

The event scared us both, and we refused to play the Ouija board afterward.

Dad was a very personable, polite, and calm man with everyone. All our friends loved him; they also loved our Mom and loved hanging out at our house.

Growing up, Mom never spoke negatively to us about our Dad. She never poisoned us or transferred any of her wounds or trauma to us. Mom respected him and required that we respect him as well. Dad did the same. We were not allowed to disrespect Mom. Because of this, we grew up with a Dad who made us feel provided for and safe.

Mom saved us from significant trauma. Yet there was an undercurrent in the atmosphere from my Mom's trauma. Even as a child, I sensed it. Fear ...

"Children, obey your parents in the Lord, for this is right." Ephesians 6:1-3 NIV

Chapter 5
Success is spelled R-I-S-K

Endless possibilities existed for a curious young child living in our beautiful village, Although I felt afraid now and then, I hadn't yet been crippled by the monster of fear. I was born to venture out to the unknown, willing to risk all to accomplish a greater goal.

One day, my brother and I were left home alone. Everyday chores were extensive. Mom always had to work hard just to provide for our daily needs. We must have been asleep, and she figured she could run an errand quickly and be back before we woke up. Or maybe someone was supposed to look in on us, I'm not entirely sure.

Whatever the case, we woke up! My brother Vince decided we needed to go down the hill to the little general store to buy a candy pacifier. We were at most two and three, but I was confident in his wisdom and agility. He was my big brother, after all. So he held my hand, and off we went down the reddish dirt road.

I remember playing in this red dirt often. Regardless of what color our clothes were, they would be partially tinged in red dirt after play.

We had to pass the home of a lady in the village called "La muda," meaning *the mute lady*. There was a lot of ignorance in the little town. Adults propagated fear of this woman by telling children that if we didn't behave, the "muda" would get us. She couldn't formulate words because she was mute or deaf. Either way, when she tried to speak, her words came out in strange grunts.

As we approached her house, my brother tightened his grip on my little chubby hand. When she caught a glimpse of Vince and me, she rushed excitedly to the stone wall fence in her yard. She began calling out to us and waving happily. We interpreted this as her wanting to "get us." She made loud, unrecognizable grunts and strange guttural noises.

We didn't't dare make eye contact with her. Instead, we put our heads down and kept a side eye on her as we tiptoed to pass her home. At the sound of her grunts, fear ran up our spine. We tucked our heads into our bodies like a turtle, shrinking to make ourselves a smaller target.

We both were sure that she wanted to kidnap us. My brother grabbed my hand tighter and pulled me past her house, ensuring we walked on the furthest edge on the other side of the road.

We were relieved when we made it past her house without being kidnapped. We later learned that she was a kind, sweet lady. Yet in our childish mind, we believed those who had warned us to behave, or she would kidnap us.

Fear is real. There is a healthy fear that keeps you from the edge of a cliff or from getting too close to flames. Fear like walking away from your mom in a large crowd when you are young or getting in a car with a stranger.

A mature Christian can have a healthy fear of God, causing us to obey his Word and walk wisely. Healthy fear brings the fruit of obedience. Obedience brings transformation and healing.

However, there is an unhealthy demonic fear that some have learned to live with. It is destructive and relentless, communicating doubt, low self-esteem, and vivid pictures of what may go wrong for you. If you listen to this fear for too long, eventually, you will believe the lies it has been feeding you. If allowed to solidify, it will cripple you and cause you to lose your peace and shrink your world. It will dry up your soul.

Fear makes you devalue your worth and your talents, eroding your willingness to take a chance at success.

Instead, there are many things that you won't do because of fear. This kind of fear is a liar.

You are a wonder, created on purpose by an incredible creator who prepared a beautiful, made-to-fit destiny for you to walk in. He intends you to blossom. He intends for you to thrive!

Fight through the present predicament you may find yourself in and dare to believe God's Love and intentions for you.

"For we are his workmanship, created in Christ Jesus for good works, which God prepared beforehand, that we should walk in them." Ephesians 2:10 NKJ

Refocus on The Goal

We soon forgot our narrow escape from being kidnapped as the familiar, ambient noises returned our focus to the prize. The colorful, sweet candy pacifiers! We walked past a few homes on our path, and a rooster crowed. In the pasture, distant grazing cows mooed. A donkey approached the barbed wire fence, watching us intently through its thick eyelashes; puffs of air came from its nostrils. It bumped the wooden post with its head and bared its teeth as it neighed at us. In my mind, it was smiling at us. These were reassuring, familiar sounds to us.

The bubbling of the stream could be heard gently in the background. Not yet in our view, the familiar sound of rushing water encouraged us onward.

As we arrived at the grouping of tall, green trees, there was the stream. We welcomed the shady, fresh, cold, misty morning air.

The scent of wet earth and fragrant plants that grew by the stream filled the morning air. Birds chirped, and water rushed and fell from level to level quickly and playfully as it found its way around rocks and boulders, then continued its race downstream.

In our childish eyes, crossing the stream seemed a daunting challenge. It looked wide and deep. Yet I felt safe. I looked to my big brother for instructions as to how to proceed. He held my hand and patiently guided me to jump from rock to rock. Tenderly saying, "Over here, mija." He helped me balance so that I wouldn't fall in. We made it across safely and managed to stay mostly dry except for our squishy, wet shoes.

The little general store was in our sights! We had finally made it. The store was set at an elevation from the street. It was surrounded by a high cobblestone sidewalk.

My brother Vince walked confidently up to the well-aged wooden counter of the walk-up window. Holding up his two fingers, he ordered, "We want two candy pacifiers."

The lady heard voices but couldn't see anyone over her counter. She had to partially lay her upper body on the counter and stretch her neck to peer over to where the voices were coming from.

She burrowed her eyebrows and tilted her head slightly, puzzled to see two little ones standing there by themselves, holding up two fingers. She searched to the left and the right; surely there was an adult somewhere.

She knew our family and where we lived. "Where's your mom?" she asked gently.

"It's just us, and we're here to purchase two candy pacifiers," my brother repeated in his best bossy voice. Never mind that we had no money. That was a minor detail. We had made the long trek to the store all by ourselves and now expected our candy.

She reached down over the counter and gave us each candy pacifier, telling us, "Go home.".

Surprised at our achievement, we held them up triumphantly with a huge grin, like a well-deserved trophy! We said "Thank you" and started our long trek home to, "the white house, up on the hill." Somehow, the way home seems shorter and less challenging. We had our sweet reward!

A bit later, the store attendant saw our mom passing by the store on her way home. She hollered, "Vince and Maria were just here by themselves."

Mom was incredulous that we had dared to make that trip by ourselves. We were only toddlers. She rushed home. Our giggles were heard even before opening the front wooden gate to the patio. She found us sitting on the floor, chatting happily, enjoying our delicious candy. Holding them up to the sun to admire their jewel-like colors in between licks. What an adventure! It was unforgettable and worth it all. We risked, and we attained our prize!

We have learned there are things to fear. But never let fear break you. Don't allow fear to prevent you from going on a "God adventure." The kind of adventure that makes life glorious, exciting, and meaningful!

Allow his perfect love to cast out all fear. If he is for you, who can be against you?

"There is no fear in love, but perfect love casts out fear; for fear has torment, and he that fears, has not been made perfect in love...." 1 John 4:18 DBT

Chapter 6
We are Body, Soul, and Spirit.

We live life mainly in the soul, what can be heard, felt, and sensed. Yet, there is a spiritual realm that is much more important. It is where all of life's "cause and effect" originates.

Our battle is not against flesh and blood but against organized evil. On our own, without Christ, we are no match for the spiritual evil that surrounds us.

Puppet masters are behind the scenes; patiently plotting, manipulating circumstances, situations, and even people open to being used. They carefully set up intricate plots against us.

We need to have knowledge of the spiritual battle. We need to be in relationship with the one who came up against this spiritual evil and defeated it for us. Jesus overcame the devil in order to rescue us from his plans of destruction. We have to give Him the authority to work in our lives and gain knowledge of Him through the Bible, His book of instructions. His mighty Word.

However, at that time we didn't have this relationship; this needed knowledge. We had not given Him our lives. We didn't seek him for instructions and direction for living our life.

We tried to be good and did the best we could with the understanding we had. This is not enough.

In these carefree, early years of innocence, we could not have seen hints of the destruction the enemy of our soul was patiently brewing. Little did we know that these two innocent kids who played, giggled, and happily enjoyed their sweets were the target of a ruthless, supernatural enemy.

"For we wrestle not against flesh and blood, but against principalities, against powers, against the rulers of the darkness of this world, against spiritual wickedness in high places. Wherefore take unto you the whole armor of God, that ye may be able to withstand in the evil day, and having done all, to stand therefore." Ephesians 6:12-13 KJV

Evil exists; all we have to do is look around, and we realize this. The devil (organized evil) uses willing human participants to harm us, whether it be strangers or, sadly, even family.

Here we were, innocently enjoying our prize candy, unaware that one day we'd fall victim to his insidious abuse.

One day, a family member would victimize my brother, and another victimized me, which caused lifelong battles for us both.

Often, many don't realize that when a child is violated sexually, it opens them up to premature lust. In doing so, it confuses them, blurs boundaries, and makes them a target for repeated violations.

The door to the evil side of the supernatural is another door opened when one is victimized. In so doing, it allows indescribably nefarious entities to draw us into bondage. Evil spirits are real; the Bible says that they come as an angel of light, but they have only one purpose: our destruction.

Alcoholism was prevalent in some of our extended family. One day, alcoholism would ruin my brother's life and nearly destroy mine.

You see, there is a great, concerted effort for our destruction. A sworn enemy that would stop at nothing until he destroyed our lives. He exists for this one purpose.

He would have to be stopped! Yet, at that time, neither I nor our family knew how to stop him. Our elders didn't discern that there was an invisible enemy at work. I'm not sure we even believed he was real.

The devil was spoken of as a fictitious character who made you do naughty, mischievous things. We were threatened with him "getting us" along with "La Llorona" (a Mexican female equivalent to "the Boogie Man") and all kinds of other superstitions. Unaware that this enemy of our soul is real, serious, vicious, and evil. One who plays dirty and kicks you when you are down. He goes for the jugular and has no mercy, Not even for innocent children.

*" The thief does not come except to **steal**, and to **kill**, and to **destroy**. I (Jesus) have come that they may have **life** and that they may have it more **abundantly**."   John 10:10 NKJ*

You may ask, "Why so devil-conscious? Shouldn't we be thinking positive thoughts?

Why all this talk of supernatural evil? Isn't all that just a bunch of superstition?" Ignoring the devil or believing he is just a myth is dangerous.

Jesus himself spoke of evil and the devil more than we realize. He warned us and exposed many of his devices. We need to know our enemy to prepare a defense.

Religion and Good Morals are not Enough.

We were blessed with a nurturing extended family. They all watched, corrected, and taught us right from wrong. To the best of their ability, they made sure we were safe. They also gave us a religious upbringing. We were taught to honor God by honoring the church, the Pope, Priests, the Saints, and the Virgin Mary. We could go to different Saints for different needs. We could even pray to our guardian angel. If you wanted your prayers answered, you prayed to Mary, who would intercede for you with her son Jesus.

Our little community had colorful festivals and fun parades to celebrate "The Virgin Mary" and the different saints. It was a very ornate and intricate religion. We were taught to reverence our religion. This is culturally expected and deeply entrenched in our entire country.

My family was very conscientious and were people with high morals. My Grandmother on my Mother's side, my "Nina Maria" in particular imparted a reverence for God to me. She made us aware of this holy being we all had to answer to.

She also imparted respect for the Ten Commandments. This gave me a strong conscience and deeply entrenched morals that drew a line that extended well into my teenage years which I couldn't cross.

I found it hard to violate my conscience, even when everyone around me was "doing it."

As a teenager, I remember my friends sporting clothes and makeup that they had stolen. When I complimented them, their response was, "Five-finger discount." Meaning they had shoplifted the items. How I wished I could steal because I sure could use some new clothes! But my conscience would not allow it. When I tried to steal, I turned every shade of red, drawing attention to myself. The store attendant instantly looked in my direction.

I had a difficult time cussing, too. I would cuss out of context and out of cadence, sounding dumb. The words didn't flow from my mouth. I had to think of them individually in my head; some didn't go together. I failed miserably at having a potty mouth, but not for lack of trying.

There are laws of nature that apply to everyone. For example, "Einstein's law of gravity."

There are also spiritual laws. "You reap what you sow" applies to everybody. Sow good things into your child. Be morally consistent. Live a good life in front of them.

This does not save them. It doesn't redeem them. Only Jesus can do that.

It will, however, build a strong conscience and foundation in their formative years. This will draw deep boundaries, making living an immoral, destructive life very hard. They can still choose to do it. They will, however, need to jump over numerous hurdles. They will have to battle their conscience and try harder than those without convictions. They will have to violate their conscience at every turn to do it.

The conscience can eventually be seared if they are persistent. If consistently violated, the conscience can be silenced. It will, however, take a lot of effort to get there. Putting every obstacle available between the child and sin is wise as a parent.

Many have the philosophy that they will not force religion on their kids. They will instead wait until the child is older and let them choose for themselves. They don't realize that they are missing a God-ordained season where children are malleable This erroneous philosophy hurts the child. Refraining from giving them a strong foundation in their formative years is a mistake.

Spiritual training is our God-given duty and responsibility. One day, we must account for how we raised our kids. Formative years make up their foundational character. Creating a solid, godly foundation in them in this season is a form of equipping them to face life better.

What one learns and practices as a small child will become the foundation on which their character will be based. They will either struggle because of these habits, beliefs, and flaws or have an advantage because of the foundational strengths they acquired in these formative years.

If you leave an adequate understanding of God out of their childhood, it will take more hardship, heartache, and suffering for them to recognize their need for God.

"Train up a child in the way he should go, and when he is old, he will not depart from it." Proverbs 22:6 KJV

Chapter 7

Our Little Family Moved to The Center Of Town.

There is an epidemic of fatherlessness in our society. A deep need within us for a father, a protector. This is true, even in this age of strategic shaming of men for being masculine. There's an attempt at removing them from their leadership role. Patriarchy is erroneously considered oppression. Strong fathers are needed.

The devaluing of their strength is damaging children, wives, and families. It is a conscious, purposeful strategy to deconstruct the family, the home, and ultimately our society. This results in harm to a child's psyche, their sense of security, and self-worth. It erodes their sense of safety, causing significant damage. This household destruction creates a loss of order inside the child's soul.

Eventually**,** we moved out of "the white house" and down from our hillside to the main street in our little village. There was only one cobblestone paved road, and we now lived on it. Our new home wasn't too far from the Catholic Church, which we could see from our front porch. It was the only church in our little village.

Most people had no watches or clocks. Time was kept by the ringing of the church bells, which could be heard echoing far and wide throughout the village and surrounding hills. People stopped, focused, and counted the gongs at the sound of the bells. They knew it was time to hurry or time to quit. The activity and rhythm of the town were closely intertwined with the church.

Early Sunday morning, Grandma Maria would don a clean apron, her light brown hair always neatly braided out of the way. She'd then charge into her kitchen, determined to tackle the day's assignments. A little while later, she could be heard whistling, and we knew she'd be on a roll and did not take kindly to interruptions.

Grandma would squint her pretty hazel eyes, lean her body in cautiously as she lit the kindling wood, and stoked her fire. She'd grab the handy bellows that hung on a nail on the smoke-stained wall and get it roaring, ready for today's meal. She placed her pot of beans or chicken soup on the clay burner that Grandpa built on top of her brightly tiled kitchen counter.

While it cooked on the open fire, she placed steaming, charred, roasted chilies, tomatillos, and tomatoes in her grinding stone "molcajete" to grind into a salsa. She also chopped cilantro, onions, and garlic for her fresh salsa. Her whistling never stopped until the church bells tolled.

My brother, our baby sister, and I played out on her Patio or in front of her house. When she heard the bells, Grandma rushed out to fetch us. "Maria, Vincente, Martha, come wash your hands."

She wrangled us like wild stallions, dipped her apron into the water bucket, and vigorously wiped our faces. She'd then dipped her cupped hand in the water bucket and sprinkled water on our sweaty heads. Smoothing out our hair with her brush. "Show me your elbows and knees," she ordered. She then proceeded to scrub them clean with her wet apron. When we were all scrubbed and ready, she removed her apron, smoothed her own hair, and announced, "Time for Mass!". Then, off we all walked down the cobblestone street toward the church. Never mind, we still smelled like sweaty puppies. We looked clean, and that's all that mattered.

By this time, my father was absent. Laborers were needed in the USA and he had gone to live and work there. Legal status was promised as an incentive to all who came to work under the "Bracero" program. Once they had been employed for a certain number of years, their families could eventually acquire legal status. Joining the long tradition of foreigners who came to the US to live in peace and, with determination and hard work, achieve the "American Dream."

Dad came home to the village on visits twice a year. He made a baby and then returned to the States. So, mom was left to raise three, four, and then eventually five kids alone.

Our extended family tried to create a safe atmosphere for us, yet I still remember living with a sense of abandonment. Although they made us aware that our Dad was away working and that he did it for us. Still, the feeling of not having our Dad was always present.

The world's most valuable commodity isn't diamonds, gold, or platinum. It's something that's within our grasp every day. Our children!"

Saturday was wash day. We walked with Mom, who would carry her round tin tub of dirty clothes to the stream. She washed and talked with other ladies who gathered to do their laundry under the cool shade of massive trees. They scrubbed and slapped the garments on their favorite rock. My siblings and I played with the other kids who also came with their moms. We splashed and giggled as we bathed in our underwear in the pools of water that formed on the sides of the full rushing stream.

When they were done washing their clothes, the ladies also bathed in their full slips and underclothes. When clothes, children, and ladies were squeaky clean, all would dress.

Moms carried their tin tubs filled with clean, damp, rung-out clothes on their hips to be hung at home on their clothesline. Their wet hair was done up in a high bun on top of their head. They all walked away from the stream in different directions, heading to their own homes.

We owned a small general store. I once overheard a family member telling Mom, "You will never turn a profit if you insist on granting everyone credit." Mom felt terrible for those who hadn't enough to eat. Kids showed up to our store with a list and a message from their parents asking, "Can we please buy some needed food staples?" Followed by "We will pay next week."

Mom never said no, and they didn't always pay. We didn't turn much of a profit, but I loved and admired my Mom's soft, compassionate heart.

It is said that you have to be taught empathy while you are still young. It is also noted that empathy must be modeled in front of you. Mom did that very well. To this day, I can't look at a suffering individual and not feel for them. This is thanks to my Mom.

Mom lived out empathy. She taught us that people matter more than things. She taught us not to repay evil for evil. Because of my Mom and Grandmother, I felt deeply obligated to this unknown, mysterious God. It was my responsibility to be a decent, caring human being.

I loved our new home. It was large and spacious, with an arched entrance and a heavy, aged wooden door fitted with old wrought iron hardware. Our bedroom's only window had no glass, simply wooden double doors and both the door and window had remnants of turquoise blue paint, making it even more beautiful.

Mom opened the window every morning and closed it every night with an iron skeleton key. Letting in the morning sunlight that filled the room and bounced off the whitewashed walls.

Our Mom was preparing to open our little general store one early morning. It was dark out, so my siblings and I still slept.

I awoke to a burning in my nose. It had become hard to breathe. Smoke filled the bedroom. My mind tried to grasp what was happening. Blinking my eyes, I focused on an amber-red glow; a flame from outside could be seen through the large keyhole of the window shutters. It resembled light reddish and blue fingers reaching in from under the shutter. It hadn't caught the wood on fire yet but was charring it black, and glowing red embers were forming on the edges.

My baby sister Norma was asleep in her crib. The canopy veil that kept mosquitoes from biting her as she slept was suspended from a hook on the window near this fire.

My brother Vince woke and was also sitting on the edge of the bed, staring in confusion at the burning window shutter. He suddenly became wide-eyed, woke my sister, Martha, and then ran to get Mom. She and an uncle ran in and quickly pulled the veil off the window, pushed the crib away with our baby sister still in it. He then put out the flame, scraping off the embers from the wood. He opened the window to air out the room. Smoke damaged the corner of the wall, and all of our belongings absorbed the smell of kerosene.

Throughout the day, I kept coming back to the room, taking in the kerosene smell, staring at the blackened wall and window to convince myself that it was not a bad dream. Someone had actually tried to burn our house down.

Family members angrily questioned, "Why would anyone do that? Who does that?" "Knowing there are children asleep in the room!" "It was intentional!"

Our next-door neighbor had rolled up a newspaper soaked in kerosene and jammed it into the keyhole. She then lit it while we were still sleeping in the room. The fact that it was malicious and intentional registered in my young mind! Why did this woman despise us so much?

On another occasion, our well was poisoned. This same neighbor had thrown a dead cat into it. In my imagination, our neighbor was a scary, shadowy monster who sat in a dark cave and thought of ways to destroy small children. I wasn't happy to live there in our new home anymore. I wished my Dad was home to protect us. I didn't feel safe. I became hyper-sensitive to sounds and smells and saw shadows in every corner. Fear was never too far away.

Surprisingly, Mom didn't rehash the event. Not wanting to instill fear in us or hate for the woman. She dropped it and moved on. I never heard my mom speak ill of this neighbor, even when she had to go elsewhere to draw clean water to cook and drink.

Many years later, while already living in the USA, I overheard Mom speaking on the phone on one of my visits to my parent's home. She was giving someone directions. "What is that all about?" I asked a cousin who was visiting. "She's getting information to go help someone," my cousin said.

It was this same neighbor who had made our life so miserable when we were little. She was in a bad situation without any resources and needed help. She approached my Mom, who willingly helped her without fanfare. That's what we grew up seeing, always.

With such examples in our lives, you would think we had every chance and opportunity to thrive and succeed. So, how did I end up in a coma, teetering between life and death on a hospital bed?

I inspected my early years for traumatic experiences, negligence, and abuse. There were isolated incidents, but never from a lack of care from our immediate family. What made me a target? Why was I susceptible to suicide?

Growing up, my life took some wrong turns. Add to that a supernatural reality, a sworn enemy we weren't aware of then.

Our religion was a religion of good works and rituals. It did not prepare me for the unseen, ever-present foe that followed our bloodline, going back to Spain, and our Indian ancestors.

What spiritual doors were opened by them? Which of our ancestors gave a legal right to the enemy to wreak havoc in our lives? Who is fully aware of the sins of the Fathers? These enemies were familiar with our family. They had an acute ability to read us and set traps we would naturally fall into. Without as much as an alarm going off in our gut, we were easy prey generation after generation.

Since living "in town," our mornings were awakened by the rhythmic clattering of horse hoofs on the cobblestones. The double doors of our little store would already be open wide, and Mom would stand behind the counter, ready for business. Those who passed by tipped their hat or nodded in acknowledgment, saying "Good morning." Mom received 30 or 40 greetings of "Buenos Dias" daily.

Cattle mooed lazily as men patiently drove the herd down the middle of our street to graze in the open fields down in the valley. Roosters faithfully announced the sunrise, and the sound of passing vendors calling out their wares mingled with it all. These were the sounds of home. They were familiar.

However, my memories are not all pleasant. There were no streetlights, and unless the moon was out, the night was very dark and eerie. When the sun went down, most families were indoors.

Not many good things happened after dark. I recall guns being shot in the air, hooping and hollering, flaring tempers, and serious gunfights breaking out.

Mom made us kids run up a ladder to hide from the flying bullets. (A long log with steps cut into it that we used to go up into our attic.)

Years later, we would tease Mom, "You know, Mom, When bullets are flying, you're supposed to hit the floor, not go up into an attic with thin walls!"

Mom tried to put on a brave face for us, but fear carries a scent; it is something that is excreted out from our pores, and instinctively, those around us sense it. Also, her eyes betrayed her effort at bravery. I imagine she was just as scared as we were.

On another occasion, my siblings and I sat playing on the floor. Loud wailing and desperate, shrill screams echoed in the air. We froze suddenly. Staring wide-eyed at one another without speaking. A woman pleading for help as her husband whipped her with his thick leather belt, up and down the street. She had done something to displease him, and he thought he was within his right to hit her. People rushed to close their windows and doors, I wondered, "Why doesn't anyone help her?" We tried unsuccessfully to keep playing our game, but our shoulders tensed with every wail. After shutting our windows, Mom took us to the back of the house with the promise of hot "Abuelita Chocolate." The screams were not as loud back there.

At such times, our beautiful brick home with white walls, bright turquoise tile floors, and wooden beamed ceilings suddenly felt cold and scary.

Fear seemed to be a constant in our lives in one form or another as far back as I could remember. "Kids are resilient" is something that we hear often. However, our little souls recorded everything, the good, bad, pleasant, and traumatic.

Dad's In Town

Dad visited every six months and only stayed for a few weeks. Everyone made such a fuss when there was word that Dad and a small group of men would be returning from the "north" (USA). Husbands, sons, brothers, and boyfriends would return home after a very long absence!

The mood of the whole village became festive, and rightly so. Families would be reunited, even if only for a short time. They usually brought much-needed finances to purchase necessities for their family to survive the following year. While these men were in town, the village was in a frenzy of activity.

The sound of the melancholy violins, the cheerful trumpets, rhythmic guitars, and the base of the "guitarron" could be heard throughout the town. The bold, romantic songs of the Mariachi serenaded at the window of some young lady who was being sought out as a prospective bride.

The saying, "Wine, women, and song," characterized the returning young men's celebration. Happy to be home, they drank until the wee hours of the following day. It was expected, and the entire town enjoyed these special days.

My Dad was very handsome; everyone said so, and of course, I believed so. He seemed like a made-up character. A superhero of sorts that we only heard about. Who we got a very short glimpse of two times a year.

On one occasion, we were told Dad, who had just arrived in town, was sitting in a room with other men. My older brother, who must have been four years old, walked in and studied the men's faces. It had been so long since we had seen our Dad that my brother asked in confusion, "Which of you is my Dad?" The men just laughed, but my brother was asking a sincere question. He wasn't sure which one of them was our Dad.

Families slaughtered chickens or hogs to celebrate our returning men who had come home for a long-awaited visit.

Their return was always timed to coincide with a national holiday, and the town "fireworks guy" was in excellent form, showing off his best fireworks. The smell of gunpowder filled the air. It wasn't rare to have a fireworks misfire, swoosh by, nearly missing you. You always knew who the fireworks guy was; he was the one with missing fingers, and his fireworks were neither "safe nor sane." Still, the cracking, sizzling, and whistling sounds piqued everyone's excitement. We knew that a loud explosive boom would follow. The bright rockets lit up the sky. Their light making it possible to glimpse the colorful decorations in the church square. Happy faces stared mesmerized at the never-ending display of bright, colorful explosions.

Then, before you knew it, the visit was over, the festivities were over, and the small town was filled with sadness. The men and our dad had to return "north." It was necessary.

Their families could not survive without the finances they sent home.

It felt like they were going to the other side of the world. There were no phones in the village, and the internet didn't exist yet. Once back in the States, they'd keep in touch through the Postal Service. Their family waited eagerly for these rare letters to arrive. They'd be read, reread, and shared with friends and family, and the whole village would learn of their content.

It was a tough time for our Mom. She has always been of small stature. She is a strong woman because she's had to be. Mom taught us to do what is right. Any sign of disrespect brought a quick, "Respect others, especially your elders!" Our Grandma was also always ready with a firm correction. "It is essential to have self-respect. So speak the truth, never steal, and show kindness and compassion to those who need it. Work hard, and don't ever repay evil for evil."

I know that we often romanticize our loved ones who have passed. However, I've realized I've been privileged to have had such a wise, levelheaded, and dignified Grandmother. My mother is cut from the same cloth.

Mom and Grandmother Maria taught us this by example. They have always been funny; their witty humor made life easier. They taught us to laugh at ourselves. Not in a cruel way but in a "life isn't as bad as you think" kind of way.

Mom often told a little story that taught her not to be greedy. It was customary in our village to occasionally share a small bowl of whatever special meal you had prepared with your mother-in-law. Mom had cooked a delicious oxtail soup with chunks of beef and vegetables. As she scooped out the portion she would take to her mother-in-law, a massive chunk of delicious beef came up. She immediately returned it to the pot, "No, that piece is for me!" She fished around the pot until she found another piece of meat less delicious-looking than the first.

Her mouth watered as she poured the steamy soup into a small pot. The scent of beef, corn, potatoes, and other vegetables filled the kitchen. She finished pouring and immediately delivered her offering. She returned quickly to eat her soup with the piece of meat that she had refused to give away.

She squeezed lemon and sprinkled fragrant cilantro into her bowl, adding just a bit of chili. She gathered her freshly made corn tortillas and sat down to enjoy her much-anticipated prize. Taking a quick, aggressive bite of the delicious piece of meat, she almost broke a tooth; it turned out to be a bone! The entire piece of meat was one large bone.

She nursed her sore tooth, laughing at herself. "It exactly resembled a piece of meat."

She told the story with a grin, "Whenever you are tempted to be selfish or greedy, remember that bone!"

Chapter 8
Everything Changes

"When she saw that he was a beautiful child, she hid him for three months. But when she could no longer hide him..."
Exodus 2:2 KJV

As babies, most of us are loved and cherished, but as we grow, there comes a time when we cannot be hidden from the outside world.

There must have been an issue with earning a living in our little village because Dad sent word informing Mom that we would have to move. I still don't remember when or how it happened. Suddenly, one day, Mom, my four siblings, myself, and most of our extended family moved to the big city, Guadalajara proper, from our beautiful village.

Oh, what an extreme change!

Simply running errands was a colossal challenge for Mom with her five kids. Sometimes, when there was an errand to run, family members would take the long trek on the bus from their "Colonia" to come help Mom with us. They couldn't always do this, though.

A woman traveling with five small children aged six to three months in a super congested bus system was a nightmare. Most streets were cobblestone, which made for an extremely bumpy ride, and the buses filled until the doors could no longer close. Then, people hung from the door handles outside of the bus. Courtesy required that men and youth leave the seats to women with little ones and the elderly. However, there were only so many seats to go around, so many times, we'd find ourselves holding on, trying to balance and not be driven out by the crowd as they pushed to exit the bus.

My brother Vince pleaded, "Mom, we all have to hold hands," he was terrified that we would lose a child. To calm him down, we sometimes held hands, and in doing so, we created a pedestrian jam. People bumped into us because we stopped the flow on the sidewalk. Luckily, strangers would see our Mom's plight and step in and help us get on or off the bus. They'd kindly defend us if someone got upset because we were in their way.

Even with the kindness of these strangers, dread filled my stomach when I knew we had to go downtown. This was a strange place, and we felt out of place.

Dad sent finances for us to move in with an aunt. She made it clear that she was not happy to have us there. It was supposed to be temporary, as our visas to move to the USA were in the final stages of completion.

My aunt's home was a beautiful townhouse on a more affluent side of town. Two-story townhomes painted in jewel-toned colors lined the street, each with its roll-up metal garage door. I was impressed by the broad, pristine sidewalks that sat high above the street. Neatly manicured grass and fully grown trees gave this neighborhood an air of exclusivity.

We sold school supplies from a small shop we owned that Mom tended to daily. Although it was connected to the main house, we seldom saw her. We kids were forced to stay up on the rooftop all day. Mom felt bad for us but knew we weren't welcome in the main part of the house.

She'd rush up to check on us often. She made lunch, brought it up, and rushed back to mind the shop. We wouldn't see her again until the evening.

We all slept in the servant's quarters located up on the rooftop.

Mom kept our three-month-old baby brother Angel with her, but the rest of us had to stay up on the roof. It took a lot of ingenuity for four kids to stay busy alone in one room. The bare, flat rooftop was connected to our neighbor's rooftops. A brick wall separated the homes. It was topped with jagged broken bottles to deter others from jumping the wall.

Sometimes, if Mom was showering or had something to do, we'd watch Angel. We'd feed him his bottle and sometimes even change his cloth diaper. My big brother Vince had us do it assembly-line style. With all of us looking on, he'd handle the most dangerous task of undoing the safety pin, then check if it was pee or poop. I would pull off the dirty diaper and clean him while the little ones kept him from twisting.

We would put tons of baby powder on him. My big brother would then pin his diaper back up. On one occasion, Vince held his chubby legs, and I had slipped his clean diaper under him, but apparently, our baby brother had been constipated. Just as we finished powdering his booty, he shot out a little poop bullet that barely missed all of us and hit the wall. The baby powder created a large cloud that filled the air and lingered there.

My siblings and I laughed so hard until our bellies hurt. We kept reliving the moment, laugh-crying. When the laughter would die down, one of us would recall the incident, and we'd all just crack up in laughter all over again!

We found humor in everyday things, but there was little to do. Having very few belongings, we found ways to entertain each other. Our creativity kicked in. We put plays together, sang, and danced to our favorite songs. We made up games and told scary stories in that small room with only one bed.

Sometimes, we wandered out of the room. Except for a large, black water tower, the roof was bare. A short border wall surrounded the section that faced the street. Sometimes, while we played up on the roof, vendors could be heard coming down the street calling out their wares. The selection was endless: fresh eggs, knives, sharpened scissors, fresh bread, homemade ice cream, and roasted corn.

The vendor we were NOT happy to hear was the "pickled pork skins" vendor. He terrified us.

We heard the creaking wheels of his tall cart, and then his loud voice echoed down the street and up to the roof. "Cuerritooos!" It brought chills down our spine! No matter what we were doing, we froze instantly at the sound of his voice! If we happened to be out on the roof, we'd quickly duck behind the wall. Peeking cautiously over to ensure that he kept it moving. We were terrified that he would stop.

The adults in our family had warned us that if we didn't behave, the cueritos (pickled pork skin) vendor would steal us and make us into cueritos. They said that's what his large tin bucket contained: children!

After he passed, we'd be exceptionally well-behaved, at least until one of our games distracted us, and we'd soon forget the close call and go back to playing!

We longed for our Mom, we'd all sit on the upper portion of the black, wrought-iron spiral staircase that went up to the rooftop, waiting for her. We'd just sit and look down into the open patio, longing to see Mom turn the corner.

Sometimes, our Aunt would go out to wash and became irritated when she saw us sitting there. She would throw up an insult or two. She called us dirty, unmannered, dumb, naughty, a nuisance and always added a threat. "You'd better not come down," or "You'd better not make any noise." I wasn't quite sure why she disliked us so much.

Mom's inner conflict was evident. How to care for us and still mind the small shop?

The house was newly built. Impeccably furnished in a midcentury modern style throughout. I don't know how or why, but I remember one morning waking up in the beautiful master bedroom surrounded by all-matching high-end furniture. I was fast asleep on the large, beautiful bed, but someone, an uncle, awakened me. He was doing something to my little body. I was half asleep and groggy. Confused and scared, I didn't understand what was happening. He was hurting me.

When he was finished whatever it was he was doing to me, he took me to the restroom—the beautiful restroom with its skylight and its beautiful dark, royal blue tile. I could usually only sneak a peak into the sunny bathroom if the door was open when our family passed it on our way outdoors.

He turned on the shower and, with a hard shove, made me get in there and ordered me to wash up. He was very unkind and harsh. I didn't understand what had just happened, but holding back my tears, I obediently washed myself. I was confused, but I instinctively knew that something terrible had just happened. This uncle was in our lives, so he came around often. The sound of his voice made me shake, I felt as if someone had socked me in the stomach and that I could not catch my breath.

Many years later, I would realize that at five years old, I had been violated sexually by that family member.

Although Dad told us he was sending our aunt finances to house us, we felt unwelcome, unwanted, and displaced the entire time we spent living in that beautiful home.

Mom closed the shop on weekends. One Sunday, she took all of us kids to the farmers market. We loved it. We were together and had open space to run around and explore. Mom bought us a small treat, a fruit, or a dessert, which we enjoyed on our way home. We skipped and laughed, running back and forth as kids do.

Suddenly, I spotted the aunt that we lived with. I ran up to her and happily shouted out her name. She turned and looked at me as though I were an insect that had just crawled out from under a rock. "I don't know who these bratty kids are." She told her friend. Then turned to me and said, "Get away from me."

She pretended not to know us. My mom felt the sting of the insult. Sadness filled her eyes. She nudged me back by the shoulder and put her finger across her lips, telling me, "Shhh."

I hurt deeply and wondered what was so wrong with us that she would deny knowing us.

This incident left me feeling unacceptable and not good enough. It was a feeling that would become familiar throughout much of my life.

Rejection is debilitating, demeaning, and such a thief! When one is free from rejection, there is no hesitation to cross the friendship bridge to the other side, confident that what we offer will bring joy to those we meet.

Rejection is corrosive. It steals our confidence and ability to carry ourselves in this world as an offering of love, a gift freely given to others. We take a second look at what we have to give and feel that no one will want it. It's defective somehow. That is precisely what began to take root that day in my five-year-old heart.

"For we are his workmanship, created in Christ Jesus for good works, which God prepared beforehand, that we should walk in them." Ephesians 2:10 ESV

A Safe Place

Our Grandma Maria and Grandpa Santiago's house was our safe haven. Grandpa was funny and a jack of all trades. He was a brick mason and once took us to see his handiwork, a beautiful ornate dome he was building for a local cathedral. We stood under it, gazing in awe at the intricate brickwork pattern he'd created. On other occasions, he resembled a mad scientist with his thick glasses and equally thick, disheveled black hair. He was busying himself inventing some electrical gadget that was supposed to make life easier for our Grandma Maria.

Mealtime was a favorite time of day. We'd all sit around Grandma Maria's large dining room table, enjoying her delicious food. Her food was a treat, but it was not the main event. At lunchtime, we kids would sit eating slowly, craning our necks to look across the street.

Grandpa worked across the street managing the tortilla mill, which was directly in our line of vision when Grandma kept the front door open. At lunchtime, like clockwork, he'd grab a big pile of fresh, hot tortillas right off the conveyor belt churning them out. He'd then rush across the street and into the house carrying his stack of hot tortillas in his bare hands, saying, "Hot, hot, hot." Then, much to our grandma's disapproval, he'd toss the pile of tortillas directly on the table and sit in his chair. His steaming plate of food was always ready. Grandma placed the tortillas in a clean white tea towel with floral needlework. He'd grab a fresh, warm tortilla in his hand and, with a downward swoop with his other palm, smoothly roll the tortilla. Grandpa never waited for his food to cool down. He ate hurriedly, then took off again back to work. We loved watching him and his predictable routine.

Grandpa loved to sit in front of the house, whittling on a piece of wood and patiently tying strings together. He looked intently through his reading glasses as he painted small details on his work of art and then proudly presented us with an acrobatic toy figurine that flipped when you squeezed two sticks together or a carefully crafted slingshot. He made flutes and toys that I have no name for; all I know is that they were fun and created by him with care just for us. One day, Grandpa approached and said, "Give me your finger." We were used to his surprises and always cooperated quickly, curiously wondering what Grandpa was up to. He grabbed my hand, taking a small object out of his front pocket. He couldn't hide his smile as he placed a silver ring on my finger that he'd made by cutting out the center of a coin. Grandpa Santiago was spontaneous, "Come on, get up; you're coming with me," he'd order in his fake, bossy, gruff voice. "Where are we going, Grandpa?" "We're going to deliver masa [dough]," he said, straining his face, carrying the giant ball of masa wrapped in white cloth and tied in a neat knot.

His mill processed maize into masa. Tortilla factories in the surrounding area purchased their dough from him, and he delivered it on his motorcycle.

The best part was when he told us, "Go wait in the corner and be ready. Whoever jumps into the boxcar as I turn the corner can go with me." We'd quickly stop whatever we were doing and scramble to the corner. Standing with our arms bent by our side and our feet spread in an "on your marks" stance. Adrenaline pumping, excitement in our belly, we were ready to chase the motorcycle and jump on.

He'd always slowed down to a crawl as he turned the corner, but we didn't know that. We were impressed with ourselves and our ability to jump onto a moving motorcycle!

Grandpa slept on the hard tile floor on a thin bed sheet. We watched from the bed and giggled, anticipating our nightly game. He'd soon begin to doze off with his turquoise blue and white 1950s radio playing music next to his ear.

My siblings and I waited patiently until his loud snoring became rhythmic. Then one of us would sneak quietly to the radio and slowly attempt to turn the knob to "off."

Grandpa Santiago would smack our hand, snorkel a few times, and hug his radio in one swift move. Then, he quickly returned to his rhythmic snoring, never waking up. No matter how hard we tried, we could never turn his radio off. Grandpa always swore that he was wide awake listening to it.

Grandma kept us all in line, even Grandpa. There was a sense of order in their home, a sense of safety. There was also laughter and joy in their home. We never had to question whether they loved us or not; it was evident.

"A merry heart does good like a medicine: but a broken spirit dries the bones."

Proverbs 17:22 NKJV

Chapter 9
Time to Immigrate to the United States

It had been a long process living without our dad as he worked in The United States legally, and we waited for our visas to be granted. But one day, our "papers" were ready. We completed the process, and then, on a beautiful sunny day, our grandpa and grandma put their daughter (our Mom) and us on the train en route to the USA. Back then, it was like saying goodbye forever.

I was small, but I sensed that my Grandpa Santiago and Grandma Maria's hearts were breaking as they watched us all board the train.

Once inside and after we found where we'd be sitting, we quickly rushed to a window. We could see them standing there dressed in their Sunday best. Grandma was a rare sight without her apron in her light pink tailored dress with tiny mauve flowers. Grandpa with his button-up white shirt tucked into his brown khakis. His thick black hair was forced into submission, combed to the side. They looked up as the train began to move, and we waved goodbye. Mom tried unsuccessfully to hold back her tears.

We arrived at the US border after days of travel on the train. Our dad picked us up in a pink and white 57 Chevy. A few brand-new white pillows awaited us in the back seat. We climbed in, and I quickly claimed one, hugging it like a new friend. Squishing my face into it, I thought, "I don't think I have ever had a soft, new pillow before." The pink and white Chevy made me wonder, "Are we rich now?" No one we knew back home owned a car, and we certainly hadn't.

My tall, dark, handsome Dad was a stranger to us; The legend that we only heard about and got to see two times a year for short visits. He had gotten used to living by himself. We didn't realize it then as kids, but he had also gotten accustomed to living as a single unmarried man. Now, here we were, five kids and his wife. He'd have a lot of adjustments to make, as would we.

Mom never spoke ill of our father, so it wasn't until our adult life that we realized that our Dad had regularly been unfaithful to our Mom.

We lived on a short gravel road in a rural part of dry, hot Parker, Arizona, in homes reserved for farm workers. Dad had applied for and gotten this house from his job. He had worked up to lead supervisor in the agricultural fields.

The row of run-down bungalows was set between a crop field in front and an irrigation canal in the back. The wooden floors were old and splintered. Our house was at the beginning of the row, so our yard had no boundary; it just went on and on. I could see now that Dad had made an effort to make the house homey for us. The windows had loud, floral curtains, making the room a bit cooler.

We had a rickety kitchen table that had to be leaned against the wall so it wouldn't fall over. Nevertheless, we were all together as a family. Mom cleaned the old house until it felt like home to us.

We sat happily on our four unmatched chairs, eating delicious meals prepared by our mom. She only ate once we were all done with our meal. The delicious scent of fresh flour tortillas filled the house, always making everything right.

However, when she made them, Mom would half whisper, "Close the front door, or else the neighborhood kids will come!" They always seemed to know when Mom made her flour tortillas. We tried to continue eating, pretending we didn't see the freckled faces pressed against the torn screen door. Eventually, one would ask for a "toe-tila, please." Of course, Mom couldn't say no, which only encouraged the behavior.

We drank from jelly jars, and none of our silverware matched. Our toys consisted of a small cardboard box that contained a few toys that all five kids had to share, which was okay because we preferred to play outside in the crazy Arizona heat anyway. That's where the real adventures could be found.

Early Saturday morning, we woke to the smell of Mom making breakfast. Our typical breakfast included eggs, potatoes, refried beans, and homemade tortillas. We had also just discovered butter, so a warm tortilla with butter and sometimes jam became a favorite snack.

Our neighbor introduced us to Corn Flakes, and from that day forward, Mom called every cereal "Cone-fleys." Many years later, one of my daughters thought Grandma was holding out on the good cereal because all she ever offered her was "Cone-fleys." She said, "Mom, Grandma has Coco Puffs, Lucky Charms, Honey Nut Cheerios, but she won't offer us any." I had to explain to her. "Sweetheart, Grandma calls ALL cereals "Cone-fleys." She IS offering you whichever cereal you'd like."

Looking out of our screen door, we could already see the rising heat waves on the horizon. We rushed through our breakfast, eager to meet with our friends and start our day. There was an irrigation canal behind our house. Digging in the sand became one of our favorite pastimes. If you dug deep enough, you'd hit wet sand.

We found shade under a tree's full, expansive branches in our backyard. We learned to be watchful, avoiding the scorpions that crawled out from under anything left sitting outside overnight. Often, our feet would fall through snake boroughs. We'd jump out immediately, hoping the snake wasn't home! I remember running into live rattlesnakes or their shed skin and rattles so often that it wasn't anything to mention.

We once went on vacation for a few days and, on our return, walked in to find a coiled rattlesnake on our living room floor. Dad had all the kids go out of the house. Seeing our dilemma, our favorite uncle went to his truck and grabbed his shotgun. He came back, shot the snake, and declared, "Problem solved," as he threw a rug over the big hole he'd made on our wooden floor.

We found ways to enjoy ourselves doing what kids do. We swam in the irrigation canals, hoping they wouldn't open the gates to irrigate the fields and thus suck us under. Families got together on special occasions, and we'd spend the day swimming in the Colorado River.

One summer, we'd already been at the river enjoying the cool water for a while. Teens hooped and hollered and egged each other on to jump off the bridge.

Adults chatted and enjoyed their alcohol and barbecue while kids splashed and played noisily. Speed boats rushed by, and no one noticed my two little sisters, who were around 3 and 4 years of age, had been picked up by the strong current. They began to float away from the pool that formed on the side of the river where everyone else was hanging out.

Thank God they were wearing life jackets.

They were pretty far down the river before a random man saw them and kept shouting, "Who's kids are they?" No one answered, so he dove in, swam after them, and brought them back.

"We saw water and then sky, water then sky." My baby sister said, crying. "We thought no one would come after us."

"I was able to save them both because they hung on to each other," explained the man.

"We just held each other's hand and went under, then came back up, under, and back up," my baby sister kept repeating.

So many people, and no one noticed these two little ones were in danger.

I feel like that's how childhood can be. Adults are busy, and teens chase the adrenalin rush in daring activities.

Sometimes, the little ones get lost in the mix. No one notices that they are in danger.

Sometimes, parents are overwhelmed by life, and it takes an outsider to notice and speak up to save these little ones. A healthy society comes alongside parents to support them in keeping children safe. Not to undermine parental rights. Simply to nurture the family unit and strengthen the bond between the parents and the children.

"Jesus said, " Let the little children come to me and do not hinder them, for to such belongs the kingdom of heaven. " Matthew 19:14 ESV

We were a funny mix of neighbors in that little section of the rural road.

Living in Mexico, we had never seen any other race, and we were fascinated by the uniqueness of the races. Black, white, Native American, and Mexicans all on this tiny dirt road surrounded by agricultural fields.

A huge white family from Oklahoma moved in and set up two trailer homes down the way from us. Their grandma called out to me one day as I played outside. I went over to see what she needed. To my surprise, she sweetly presented me with a little cradle for my doll. She'd made it from a bleach container and some pretty yellow, floral fabric that she'd gotten from a flour sack.

I thought it was simply beautiful!

The kids were our friends one day, then wanted to fight us the next. They were a tight family. So, if you messed with one, you messed with them all! One day, one of the older boys was picking a fight with my brother Vince. We had been taught not to fight. So my brother was holding back, keeping his temper.

The boy was calling him a chicken. I couldn't hold back anymore, so I butted in and said, I'll show you who's chicken!" I kicked the boy and made him cry. Then, my brother grabbed me by my ponytail and pulled me all the way home. He said, "Don't you ever defend me!" Mom heard me crying (the whole neighborhood probably heard me) and wanted to know what was happening. My brother explained to her angrily, "She defended me and made me look weak!" I learned that day that boys don't like girls fighting their battles. Neither do men. Real men don't, anyway.

A black family moved into one of the other four homes allotted to farm workers. Their grandpa and grandma went out in their overalls and straw hats and quickly set up a vegetable garden in the sandy backyard. I felt sorry for them working hard out in the hot sun. I thought, "Nothing can grow there." Imagine my amazement when vegetation began to spring up!

I didn't enjoy helping them dig out the weeds, but I loved watering and picking vegetables. We were happy to eat whatever their Grandma cooked up with the harvested vegetables. Stuff I wouldn't have otherwise eaten, but somehow, because it was what we harvested, they were delicious!

I loved hanging out at my friend's house. Three generations in one house. Grandpa enjoyed playing the harmonica, his eyes twinkled as all of us kids joined in, laughed, and danced a jig to the music. Everything felt foreign and intriguing. I especially liked what I called "hairdo day." The scent of the hot comb filled the smoky air as my friend's older sister pressed her hair. I watched with amazement as her fingers moved rapidly, working, twisting small portions of hair forming intricate braids.

My friend and her sisters were just as curious as me; they were fascinated with my "silky" hair and always wanted to touch it.

On one of my visits, they decided to do my hair. They created their masterpiece and proudly sent me home with about fifteen tight braids.

On my walk home, I skipped happily and twirled my head back and forth, loving the clacking sound of the colorful, plastic barrettes hitting each other. I felt fabulous!

When I walked into the house, my mom smiled with amusement. "Mom, when school starts, can you please do my hair like this?" I asked, shaking my hair to hear the clacking of the many barrettes.

"With five kids and a house to keep, I think two ponytails is my limit," Mom replied. "Well, what she actually said was, "Estas loca?" but pretty close.

Shame & self-hatred.

The search for love and acceptance is universal. We all long to be understood, fully embraced, and deeply loved. I remember reading about Babies that were raised by the State in a communist country. The nursery attendants gave them the best nutrition and made sure they were in a clean environment. They were stimulated physically and intellectually. However, the nursery workers were discouraged from making loving human connections with them. As a result, the kids were small and unhealthy. They had mental anxiety and were behind in their development. Love is an essential human need, and we cannot thrive without it.

Our first source of love and acceptance is our parents. However, they may be lacking in the ability to love. They may be in a crisis. They may be wounded, cold, angry, and bitter, searching for something to soothe their own wounds, and some may succumb to substance abuse and addictions.

Rejection becomes cyclical. Mom was rejected, so she rejected you. She was neglected, so she neglected you.

Another source of rejection is rejection by our social group. If you are different in any way, you will most likely be rejected, and again, we crave that acceptance.

Rejection leaves us wounded, feeling isolated & unworthy. The person rejecting you often has no clue that they are wounding you. Other times, they are fully aware and lack empathy.

God says He will accept us! His love goes deep into the recesses of our hearts. No one else can touch the depth of our need like Jesus can!

Without God, we are left with emptiness and a deep yearning for love and acceptance. It is such a deep need that we will do almost anything to fill this need.

Perhaps we've not considered that God has the same deep yearning for us.

"The LORD has appeared... to me, saying, "Yes, I have loved you with an everlasting love: therefore with loving kindness have I drawn you!" Jeremiah. 31:3 NKJ

Chapter 10
The Dog Was Vicious

I walked down the gravel road with my older brother early in the morning. It was the 1st day of school. With a fresh, clean dress and my hair combed back so tightly that my eyes could barely close. OK, I exaggerate, but not by much. Mexican moms are known for their talent in hair combing torture.

We were on our way to the home of one of our few neighbors. They were doing our mom the favor of letting us walk along with them to the bus stop on the main highway. When we reached their front yard, my brother called out his name. Out rushed a dog barking loudly and viciously. He was vicious in my mind anyway. My big brother, who was supposed to be watching me, ran like a coward as the vicious Chihuahua dog latched onto my ankle. I shook him loose and limped home, crying and yelling loudly for my mom. In Spanish, it would be, "Ammmaaaa!" sounding similar to an ambulance siren. Blood ran down my ankle with every step, staining my ruffled white sock.

Instead of attending my 1st day of school, I went to the Dr. to receive a painful tetanus shot. That, my friend, was supposed to be my first day of school in America.

When we finally made it there the following week, we found school to be a strange, intimidating place. All the kids stared at my brother and me, and I mean "all." Curiosity, I suppose. We didn't understand a word of what the teacher or the kids said. Overwhelmed, I would hide behind the buildings at recess. Both my brother and I were timid. Sadly, the two brave little ones who dared to travel alone down the hill to buy two candy pacifiers were gone.

Not understanding the world around us made this timidity much worse.

There was a girl named Edna, yup, I still remember her name, who would find me hiding behind the building, and without saying a word, she would stand very close to me and pinch me.

Back home, after a long day at school, Mom regularly asked, "How was school today?" My brother Vince and I responded in unison, "Gooood." It wasn't; however, "good" was always our reply.

Why do kids not speak up? Maybe because they feel the tension and the stress already on parents and there is a protective side that doesn't want to put more on them. So the reply was simply, "Good!" and that was the end of that. One less thing for Mom to worry about.

She also asked my brother and me, "Is your teacher nice?"

"Yeees!" we both answered. "What's your teacher's name?" "Her name is Cheecho," we replied.

"Cheecho? What an ugly name these American teachers have!" concluded Mom.

We later realized that the kids raising their hands calling out "Cheecho, Cheecho!" were actually saying "Teacher, Teacher," but to little Mexican ears, it sounded like "Cheecho."

Trauma In Our New Country

I loved the fresh air and the early morning sunlight. It was not yet "Arizona hot" on our trek to the bus stop. Mom and the three little ones watched my brother and I from our front porch. We walked down our short gravel road together, then made a left at the end of the agricultural fields. We were visible even as we walked up the long dirt road that led to the main highway. We wouldn't't be out of Mom's view until we got close to the bus stop.

We were kicking up small clouds of dirt with our feet, laughing and taking time to get a ripe pomegranate from a branch that overhung an old fence. When we reached the bus stop, our feet were covered in dirt, and our hands were stained with the sweet, red pomegranate juice that ran down our arms.

We talked and played with the other kids waiting for the bus from our area.

Then, all at once, some of the kids stopped playing. Something had gotten their attention. I looked in the direction where they were turned and noticed a police car slowly coming up the road. It stopped near us, and a big, burly officer got off, asking our names. He seemed to already have my brother and me in mind.

We told him our names, and he said, "Come with me." He asked us to follow him and led us to the patrol car in front of our bewildered schoolmates. I spotted our Mom with our baby brother on her lap. Our two little sisters sat beside her in the back seat. Why was our mom under arrest? Were we all going to jail?

I'm unsure if I started first or my brother, but soon we were both crying. "Mom, tell him not to put us in prison!" "Please tell him we are legal!" Our siblings, who had been calm when my older brother and I first got in the car, soon joined our loud cries.

It must have been a sight to behold five kids crying at the top of their lungs. It sounded like terrible singing.

We cried, "Mom, tell him we are good; we didn't do anything wrong!"

Our small, harmless-looking mom tried calming us down, "It's okay, Okay, calm down, you are scaring the little ones!".

All sorts of terrible possibilities and scenarios flashed through my head. Thankfully, the police officer finally figured out this was a false report. He took us home with an apology. We missed school, and needless to say, we were all traumatized.

I hid whenever I saw a Police car go by for a long time afterward.

We didn't know it then, but one of our neighbors called the immigration on us. We were legally in the US, and she knew it.

This United States "north" wasn't what I expected at all. I missed our grandparents and our lush, beautiful village. I missed weaving crowns from wildflowers, making pottery from the abundant red clay, and making dolls out of corn cobs and whistles out of pumpkin vines. I missed climbing trees to pick the abundant fruit that grew everywhere. I missed riding on horseback. I missed knowing everyone whom I encountered. I was homesick; my heart ached for the familiar. I did not like living here.

    School eventually became fun; my brother and I loved learning. One day, a huge Mexican family showed up at school. They were bold and boisterous and happy. Not timid nor intimidated like my brother Vince and I were when we first arrived. Before you knew it, they had all the students of all ages and ethnicities playing Mexican games on the field. Active games that required running and chasing each other, similar to "Red Rover, Red Rover." Games that required holding hands, forming lines on opposite ends of the field. We sang loudly across the field, calling out at one another. Laughter and joyful shouts echoed throughout the school. We all held hands, formed a circle, ran to the left, then quickly to the right. All the while, we were laughing hysterically, trying not to fall. It was so much fun!

    We were unaware that we were being watched. Great concern arose among the faculty. A discussion had formed because the games we played were in Spanish!

    Suddenly, a handful of teachers approached sternly and broke us all up. With serious faces, they informed us, "You must stop these Mexican games! It's against the rules to speak Spanish in school, and if you are caught speaking Spanish, you will be punished."

    Although I'm sure this wasn't their intent, this event affected me deeply. I'd forget and was often reprimanded and punished for speaking Spanish. Because Spanish was such an integral part of my identity, this resulted in shame.

Eventually, I became ashamed of my accent and then my skin color. I felt ashamed to be Mexican. I reasoned, "These respected teachers disapprove so strongly; surely it is not good to be Mexican."

It's tragic that being so young, I would lose my self-esteem and sense of belonging in society. When I was around unfamiliar people, I remember making myself small. I tried to take up the least room possible and felt defective and wrong simply because of my race and nationality.

With time, our family fell into a rhythm, and we adapted. My brother and I attended school and learned English. Eventually, a colorful truck with a wooden schoolhouse camper came every morning to pick up one of my little sisters for kindergarten.

Mom kept the house and cared for my siblings and me. However, in the summer, she also went to work in the fields. She'd return exhausted. I remember her peeling her shoes and clothing off of her sunburned, sweaty body. Dad went to work in the fields. He mainly drove heavy machinery at this point, providing a good salary.

We are all traveling unknown territory. Today is a day we have not encountered before and will never experience again once it is gone. Do you know Jesus? If you do, please don't hesitate to tell struggling mamas about him. She is overwhelmed. Prayerfully communicate His message of hope and love. The family needs to be taught about a living Savior who cares about them and wants to be by their side to help fight their battles. We didn't know this because no one had ever told us. Life is a tough, cold place without the knowledge of Him.

"Teaching them to observe all that I have commanded you. And behold, I am with you always, even to the end of the age." Matthew 28:20 NKJV

Chapter 11
Cesar Chavez and The UFW

We began hearing conversations from our Dad about all the injustice at work and how much the farm workers were suffering. Toxic pesticides, illness, death, and unsafe working conditions were topics discussed at length at the dinner table. Cesar Chavez and the "United Farm Workers Union" became an obsession that Dad was passionate about. Predictably, Dad joined the Union. Before long, he was offered and accepted a position as a Union Regional Director in the Imperial Valley.

This changed the trajectory of our life. He went from working in agriculture and started working in an office. He took a significant pay cut, and the lack of finances was very apparent in our home. He was fighting for farm workers' rights and readily accepted the sacrifice. Our family had to tighten our belts and make ends meet with a very meager budget.

Our parents seldom explained their decisions to us, so we never knew the why for these significant changes in our family life.

Dad becoming a Union Director meant moving from our Arizona home to an El Centro, CA, apartment complex. In this complex, we met many people living in dysfunction." Are we poor now?" I wondered as we entered our nearly empty apartment.

The living room had no furniture, and we had our meals on a dining room table that someone had given us. Our parents had a double bed, and the 'kids' room had two twin beds and one folding cot, which my older brother decided to stick in the huge walk-in closet where he created his private space. Other than that, the house was empty. The complex was vast. Some portions of it felt seedy; other parts felt family-oriented and safe. Our mom was diligent in keeping us safely away from bad influences.

Once again, we were the new kids in the neighborhood and school. Everyone else knew each other. The teachers knew the students; they had also taught their older siblings. They'd grown up around the same neighbors. Familiarity, a place to belong, how I longed for this. Yet it was not to be.

Within the year, we moved again to Calexico. Calexico was a small, hot, predominantly Mexican border town. The people there were proud of their heritage and language; speaking Spanish was necessary. We were mocked for speaking with a "White accent," and the kids said we were trying to be "White."

We had to work hard to relearn Spanish. Although it was our language of origin, we had forgotten much of it because we had been forbidden to speak it. We even spoke English at home to one another, only speaking Spanish if Mom didn't understand. We had to pronounce the names of cities, streets, and surnames with the correct Spanish accent and roll those "Rs." With some effort, we finally managed it.

By the time I was in 5th grade, I had developed physically too quickly. As a consequence, this placed me in situations that were way over my head. I drew unwelcome attention from older guys, and because of this, I also drew negative attention from older girls. Sometimes, life got rough; I tried to be tough and not let myself be pushed around.

This new apartment complex was nice, well-kept, and spacious, The units were actually townhouses. We were practically all latchkey kids; the families were normal, with caring parents, but the teenagers were free to act up until their parents came home from work.

One day after school, my friend came to my door, "My sister wants you." A bit curious as to why, I said, "OK," and followed behind her to where her sister awaited. There were also some older guys standing around. She was standing on the porch, "What's up?" I asked.

"I heard you think you're tough!" she said. She then started cussing at me.

I was completely taken off guard. I never even spoke with her; I just knew she was my best friend's older sister. So, I was completely blindsided and didn't know how to react. She jumped on me, quickly knocked me down, and began to punch me in the face; I was shocked and froze.

They had been having a conversation in which my name came up, and the next thing I knew, here I was. At some point, the guys pulled her off me, laughing because I wasn't even defending myself. She kept cursing at me as I walked away. I turned and saw the guys still laughing; even my friend was laughing.

I walked back to my house, still bewildered. Getting beat up by an older girl because the guys had told her she couldn't do it was humiliating.

I determined to toughen up and not let that ever happen again. Even when you didn't look for trouble, trouble always found you.

No one had yet told me that connecting to Jesus would give me clarity and strength. A narrow road to follow that would give my life direction and purpose, or that a relationship with Jesus would guarantee my salvation. So I flailed around in insecurity, going where the wind blew me. The enemy of my soul set up traps for me, and I just walked right into them without a clue of what I needed to be aware of.

"I am the vine; you are the branches. Whoever abides in me and I in him, he it is that bears much fruit, for without Me you can do nothing." John 15:5 NKJV

Chapter 12
My First BFF

Calexico is where I met my first "best friend." We were both the tallest girls in our class at school. We thought we were cool in our hip huggers, thick leather belts, bell bottoms, corduroy pants, and desert boots, and our frizzy, wavy hair parted in the middle. We enjoyed going to the community pool and riding around hanging on the "sissy bar" of a friend's bike.

We caught the tail end of the hippie days, but we were teenyboppers, so we were into pop bands and teen idols. Buying the latest 45 records of Michael Jackson or Donny Osmond, then rushing home to listen to them on her record player.

My BFF and I secretly still played with Barbies and her "Easy Bake Oven." But we were also tomboys. Like once lying to Ponyboy, telling him that we knew how to ride his dirt bike, then speeding by him, going around and around hollering, "How do I stop?".

"American Pie" was the song of the year. There was a terrorist attack carried out at the 1972 Summer Olympics in Munich. Apollo took its last trip to the moon, and I was finally beginning to feel American.

We played softball in the field behind our apartments and soccer at school. We were silly together. She was always carefree and fun; I believed she was "lucky" because she was better off financially than me, but none of that mattered. We were BFFs. I once went to her house after school and met her large family. They had a nice, comfortable home.

Then, one day, I was surprised that they were moving to our apartment complex, right across the courtyard from me. I remember being in her apartment the day some beautiful floral carpet was added to their stairs. Unlike our sparsely furnished apartment, they actually had furniture. I loved her home, and I thought it was "fancy."

We loved roller skating and played roller derby any chance we got. We'd rush home, throw our school books down, kick off our shoes, and lace up our roller skates. Then out we went with the other kids. The expansive apartment grounds had a sidewalk in the inner courtyard. It was shaped in a figure 8, perfect for roller derby.

We flew by the neighbor's front porches, trying to catch one another. When we did, we'd elbow each other, pushing one another off the Figure 8 sidewalk. You were lucky if you were shoved to the left because then you'd end up on the grass. But if you were shoved to the right, you ended up in the bushes.

We became excellent skaters and loved the wind in our faces and rushing through our hair, speeding up and leaning into the turn, bending our knees, and crossing one foot over the other, making that sharp turn successfully was so satisfying. We seldom took our skates off. When hungry or thirsty, we'd quickly stomp into the house and go to the faucet to grab water or a sandwich before our moms could shout, "Get out of this house with those skates!" I had old skates with metal wheels someone had given me. I loved them.

One day, my best friend came to show me her brand-new white skates that had come in the mail. When she brought them out to show me, they seemed to glow. The wheels were chunky, made of rubber, clean, and perfect. I had never seen brand-new skates before. They were not perfect and clean for long, though. Soon, we were out there putting them into action. Our days were spent just having fun. Unless we had some unfinished homework to attend to, we stayed out until the sun went down.

School was also fun, and I loved playing sports; I got pretty good at soccer, the favored game there.

I did well in my studies and loved my teacher. He taught us many songs from every era of history. He also taught us classic poetry. I memorized "Stopping by Woods on a Snowy Evening" by Robert Frost, "The Charge of the Light Brigade" by Alfred Lord Tennyson, "Pocahontas" by William Makepeace Thackeray, and many more. He awakened in me an interest in the arts. I enjoyed sketching and painting, needlepoint and sewing. I loved this teacher, and I did my best in his class. He was a very caring man, and there was something different about him. I couldn't put my finger on it, but there was a special atmosphere in his classroom. I remember feeling safe there.

One day, I was in my class, and another student approached me and said, "There are two girls here from high school. They came here to kick your butt." The student, of course, used different language. The two girls were waiting for me outside of my class. Most students had left, but I was cleaning the desktops for Mr. Coughlin. They passed by and looked in. Our eyes met, and I got that familiar ache in my gut. That sinking feeling you get when you realize that the world is a dangerous place.

Somehow, my teacher knew something wasn't quite right. He asked, "Are you okay?". "Yup," I avoided his eyes and proceeded to put away the sponge and cleanser in the cupboard. "Would you like to stay and wait in class until they leave?" he insisted. "I'll be okay." I looked at his compassionate eyes and waved insecurely as I walked out into the outdoor corridor.

Truth be told, I was scared, but I wouldn't let them intimidate me.

I proceeded outside, focusing on my peripheral vision, my heart pounding. They weren't outside the classroom anymore. I continued walking tentatively through the corridor, slowing down before any large shrub or before I turned a corner. Then I found myself off school grounds.

So I headed toward home. On the way, I saw a large, solid tree branch. I picked it up and swung it around several times to see if it would make a good weapon. I rested the branch like a bat on my shoulder and started for home, determined that I wasn't going down without a fight. The girls were waiting off campus. They saw me and started threatening me from a distance. I didn't recognize them; they mentioned a guy's name that was in the Folkloric Dance troop, which I had just joined. He wasn't even aware I was alive; I didn't know their problem with me. The other kids walking home heard what was going on and slowed down, waiting to see what would happen.

"Come on," I said, swinging the branch. In my head, I was saying, "Don't come on!" But I couldn't show fear. They followed me, shouting curse words at me. When they realized I wasn't an easy target, they threatened me again and left.

We must have gotten loud because the crosswalk lady told my little sister afterward, "You should have seen your sister; she is crazy." "She was about to give some older girls a beat down." I was scared but had learned the hard way that you cannot show fear. Later, when Mom came home tired from working all day, and asked, "How was your day today?" The answer would be "Good," the same as when we were small.

My Red New Testament

I remember my teacher, Mr. Coughlin, with his big, wide, brown wingtip shoes. He was very kind and seemed to know all the turmoil in my young soul. I was a latchkey kid. That day that those two girls came to beat me up, I feared facing them. Strange enough, courage rose within me after he offered his help. Mr. Coughlin "saw" me, "heard" me. Not many people did. It was soothing to the soul.

What came to mind that day on the way home was that Mr. Coughlin was different. What was that big brown leather book that sat open on his desk when we returned from recess? He didn't say much, but his blue eyes were filled with kindness.

One day, he had a guest come and share the gospel with the class. I don't remember what was said. But I remember the guest lifted a red New Testament at the end of the presentation and asked, "Who wants one?" All the children raised their hands and shouted, "Me, me, me!" Although I had not grasped or understood what was said, I also raised my hand, but before the guest was able to pass out the bibles, Mr. Coughlin said, "Wait, you can only get one IF you promise to read it." We, of course, all promised we would, and each received one.

I happily showed it to my Mom when I got home. She told me, "It's not a real Bible because it's not Catholic." I wondered if she was right because, trying to keep my promise to Mr. Coughlin, I tried to read it every night for days, but It made no sense! Defeated, I put it away.

Calexico was a wholesome small town back then, and we thrived there. My brother joined the football team. I remember being hopeful in junior high and believing my future was bright if I applied myself, kept my nose clean, and worked hard. I truly tried. I was studious; I tried to mind my parents. I revered the God I'd learned about from my mom and Grandmother. Yet even though I was doing well in my studies, being involved in the student body, going out for cheerleading, and associating with the right crowd, I was fighting a losing battle. I didn't know that there were spiritual forces against me that were stronger than me, against whom I had no defense.

Dad was completely enmeshed with Cesar Chavez and the Farm Workers movement. We participated in boycotts, went to the jails, and sang to those arrested while boycotting. They could hear us through the windows and shouted back funny comments in response. It was not a sad atmosphere; they were proud to suffer for the cause. But we did witness sadness and serious, heartbreaking situations.

One December, someone had tried to burn my Dad's offices down. We went to see what was left and were relieved they had only managed to burn down one room. Sadly, it was the room where toy donations were being stored. I remember the pungent smell of smoke and the melted, burnt toys that the children of farm workers were supposed to receive for Christmas. A small pile of rescued toys lay by the door; although these were covered in smoke, they were not charred. Our younger sisters and baby brother got one toy each from this pile. These toys were scrubbed clean yet still smelled like smoke, even months after.

We weren't told directly what was happening, but we would overhear the adult's conversations. We learned that the Union had many enemies.

One evening, the adults were around the kitchen table talking in hushed tones. You could pick up on the tension in their quick conversation and the alarm in their voices. They all spoke at once. Some had tears in their eyes. "What happened?" I wondered but didn't dare ask any of the adults. We kids just watched from the other room. Phone calls and plans were being made swiftly. We began to get the full picture of what had happened. A bus carrying farm workers out to work in the fields overturned into a canal, and because the bus seats were screwed down with flimsy, cheap screws, the seats broke free and crushed the farm workers, and 19 drowned or were crushed to death. The news was overwhelming; we had seen some of these people not long before, and now they were dead.

A mass funeral was held for the victims of this tragedy in a very large hall. My family and I were up on the platform with Dad and other Union leaders, so I had a view of the entire hall. It was filled to overflowing. Grief & anger made the air thick and suffocating, and caskets draped in black Union flags were lined up neatly in the dimly lit room.

Men wore black funeral bands around one arm. There were speeches given from the podium, and the unfair treatment and unsafe working conditions were discussed passionately. Hearing the "Us against them" rhetoric became a bit scary. Some threatened violence and vengeance, but Cesar Chavez always calmed the room down. Living through this experience impacted my young mind. I was left with the impression that a Mexican's life was less valued than other races.

When our Dad took us boycotting along the grape vines up in Northern California, the farm owners carried rifles and guns and made sure the Union workers saw them. Danger and tension were apparent. The striking farm workers marched on the sides of the fields, pumping their boycott signs in the air and shouting slogans. They were perfectly aware that the threats and danger were real.

We were made aware of the reasons for boycotting. We remember hearing about "the grapes of wrath," chemicals causing farm workers cancer.

There was a fight to lengthen the handle on the hoe used by the farm workers. The short hoe was used because it would not harm the crop, yet caused permanent damage to the farm worker's back. Most could no longer work by the average age of

45. These issues and many more were regularly heard in our home, and the Union was all-encompassing in our lives in this season.

We were in the thick of things; we went to DeLeno to the Union Headquarters, where Dad met with Cesar Chavez and the other leaders. Cesar also stayed at our house with his German Shepherds, "Red and Huelga," I believe were their names. We weren't allowed to tell anyone that he was there. He was accompanied by his bodyguards who stood guard outside, in their cars, and some in the house, by our doors and windows. We were told that men wanted Cesar dead, so we could not tell anyone he was in our home.

Dad instructed us not to bother Cesar, But Cesar would always direct some friendly conversation our way. There came a time when he seemed all consumed with weighty decisions, and we heard afterward that he was on a protest fast.

Dad was always gone, working; we only saw him for dinner, and then it was bedtime. He seemed distant.

Chapter 13
Mom Steps in and Saves the Day

We lived with bare necessities. Our home was large but sparsely furnished until Mom began working. She immediately started buying things for our home. We were overjoyed when a truck dropped off a brand new, beautiful orange sofa with its matching recliner. We proudly invited our friends in to see it.

We even had a tree that Christmas, and Mom wrapped and placed some gifts under it. My brother picked up a round present wrapped securely with green Christmas wrapping and topped with red bows. We laughed as he bounced the fully wrapped gift on the floor and asked sarcastically, "I wonder what this is?" It was obviously a basketball that Mom had wrapped.

That Christmas, she watched with pride, her eyes filled with joy, as we each opened one brand new, store-bought gift.

Early Sunday mornings, my tiny Mom would load all of us kids into Dad's old, red Chevy truck. We would look at her curiously because we had only seen her drive out in Arizona in the empty fields, where it was safe; there was nothing to hit. She had a determined face, and even though she sat on a pillow, she could barely see over the dashboard or reach the gas pedal. Looking into the truck, you may have supposed it was only filled with children. Nevertheless, we all sat in the front seat, ready for our adventure and filled with excitement. It's sort of like when you are about to jump off an airplane. With her five kids dressed in their Sunday best, we'd head off for church.

    She'd sometimes side-swipe parked cars as she drove down the narrow, tree-lined streets. We kids would hear the scraping noise but weren't sure if we heard what we thought we heard. Looking towards Mom, she would not flinch. She sat as straight as a board and just kept her eyes on the road without flinching. So, after a while, we followed suit. When Mom sideswiped a car, we all just looked straight ahead and never mentioned it. We are sure there were numerous cars all over town with red paint scrapes on the side from our Dad's red Chevy truck.

    After Mass, Mom took us to "Jack in the Box." We'd sit on the hard, plastic, white chairs and excitedly wait as Mom ordered food. When the order was ready, we'd already divided our ketchup packets and sat with our hands clasped, mouths watering as the scent of burgers filled the air. She always bought the same thing: three Jumbo Jacks with everything! Which she would then cut in half to be shared between two siblings. If Mom had extra money, she'd also order onion rings, which she shared with us. We would get two onion rings each. What a treat!

    If a good movie was playing on Saturday, she would buy us food to share. Then, drop us all off at a movie with instructions, "You two older kids are responsible for the little kids." We'd come into the theatre maneuvering the crowd with the younger kids in tow and holding on to our food. Search for a row that all five of us could fit into. We all sat quietly for a few hours, transported to another place as we enjoyed the movie and the food. I vividly remember watching "Willie Wonka and The Chocolate Factory."

After a while, we began to notice no one else our age would have to babysit their brothers and sisters. We'd glimpse some of our schoolmates running wild in the theatre. We started wishing we could hang out with them.

Mom was a nurse in the Farm Workers Union's Free Clinic. The farm workers were mainly Hispanic. The volunteers were predominantly white and from affluent families. The medical staff was excellent. They took up the farm workers' cause and did whatever they could to help. Most of them were college educated hippies. They became part of our social circle. We loved hanging out with them.

Dr. Ken inspired me to be a nurse. That became my calling and career goal; I was sure of it! I confidently told anyone who would listen, "I am going to be a nurse and work with Dr. Ken." I'd often stop by the clinic after school on my way home and hang out.

One day, Dr. Ken called me into the room to be his nurse and assist him in treating a wound. He made me scrub down and put on a paper gown, gloves, and a mask. He asked me to hand him the giant swab as he flipped the triangle-shaped skin flap on the patient's knee, exposing the meaty insides of the wound. He then poured disinfectant on it and swabbed it. I began to feel lightheaded, and my knees were weak. He asked me to hold the patient's knee still as he flipped the skin flap back and began to suture it together. I watched the needle go into the skin, and the way it pulled as he tugged at the thread caused my lightheadedness to increase. He asked me for something else, but his voice sounded distant. At this point, I ran out of the room to vomit. I was dry heaving in the bathroom and could hear Dr. Ken's voice, "Hey, what happened to my nurse?" The nurses giggled, saying, "I think she decided she wants a different career!".

  My Mom was very well trained in patient intake; she took temperatures, blood pressure, and weight and helped the patients fill out the forms with all the familiar questions. We had good friends, hit our stride, and started to feel we were part of a community. It felt wonderful!

  One day, Dad suddenly went away. Months afterward, Mom was in the kitchen on the house phone. "Vince, come here. Your Dad wants to talk to you." We had been running in and out of the house, playing with our friends. Vince got on the phone with Dad. Something in his voice made me stop and listen. He reasoned with Dad about something. "Dad, I'm on the football team; please, Dad, can't we stay here? We don't want to leave." He was pleading, and I heard the desperation in his voice. Mom told him, "Give your sister the phone." I took the receiver, and Dad told me he had found a house for us and got a job in El Monte, California. We would be leaving within a week. "Dad, please, can't we just stay? I am getting good grades; I'm in the student body," I couldn't hold back the tears. "Dad, I'm a cheerleader, we have friends" I felt a knot in my throat and a wave of panic. Dad told us it was something that had to be done.

He hung up, and my brother and I turned to our Mom and began pleading with her, "Mom, please tell Dad we can't move," "We love it here, Mom, please."

It was no use. Everything was ready, and we would join him within the week. Dad had grown tired of never quite having enough finances to live on while he worked for the Union, so he had moved to Los Angeles ahead of us to find employment and a home to live in.

Soon enough, we had a moving truck in the back of our home. Our friends watched sadly as we filled it up and got in. We had told them we were moving to "El Monte," so we thought we were moving to the wilderness in the mountains.

We hugged them, promising never to forget them. Waving goodbye, we watched them get smaller and smaller until they were gone from our view and from our lives.

We only saw what was visible. If we could have seen into the invisible, we would have seen dark, ominous clouds gathering above us. We were stepping into plans and strategies carefully crafted and formed against us.

But one day, the light would shine on me, and the darkness would have to flee!

"The light shines in darkness, and the darkness has not overcome it." John 1:5 NIV

Chapter 14
Culture Shock… Again

We moved from our small, sleepy town, where teens still had chip-and-punch parties. The boys huddled in a group on one side of the room and threatened to ask the girls to dance but never did. Then, on the opposite side of the room, the girls giggled in their flat shoes, wearing cute barrettes in their hair. All the while, vigilant parents chaperoned and ensured we were all safe. It doesn't mean we didn't sneak around and push the limits. However, there is something to be said about parents who actively monitor kids and have strict boundaries.

And now we moved to a city known to be a "bad environment" for kids - into substandard apartments. Dad knew it, but it was what he could afford just coming out of the UFW Union. Apologetically, he said, "It's only temporary until I get myself situated."

The youth my age that I met had lost their innocence. It was new territory, and it felt risky and dangerous.

As a young woman, my Mom had gone to school to be a tailor and was very talented. On her own time, she made men's suits, wedding dresses, bridesmaid dresses, etc. If you stayed the night and didn't have anything to wear. She'd whip something up for you on her sewing machine in no time.

She could have gone into business for herself, but there were no resources to begin a business. So, she went to work as a seamstress at a factory that manufactured men's suits. One day, Mom came home and announced, "Today I measured "la sorda" (the deaf one) because I'm making five custom suits."

"Big deal," I thought. "Who is this deaf person she measured?" It wasn't until 20 years later that I asked her, "Mom, who was that deaf person you made five suits for?" After some back and forth, she realized what I was talking about. "It wasn't a deaf person," she laughed, "It was Tommy Lasorda, the Dodger's manager!" "Ah, no wonder you made such a fuss." Something got lost in the translation!

Some of our family members who lived there in Los Angeles met up with us and took my mom and us kids to the movies—trying to familiarize us with our new surroundings. I still remember because the movie we saw was "The Exorcist" of all things! I was never the same after seeing this movie.

A day afterward, my aunt invited me to spend the night. As I slept, I kept feeling someone behind me. It felt creepy, and I was afraid to look. At other times, I felt people around me were evil and that they would be manifesting at any minute. I feared opening my curtains because I was sure someone evil was standing directly outside my window. I always felt something dark following right behind me when I walked down our long driveway.

This caused me to lose my peace; I became very fearful. Strangely enough, though, at the same time, I became addicted to watching grizzly, inappropriate movies. I also always read my monthly zodiac and was strongly drawn to dark, supernatural things. I felt a pull towards anything New Age.

The New junior high I went to was predominantly white. The few Mexicans in the school who befriended me were gang-affiliated. The school year had already started, so I was the new girl... again. I felt all eyes on me the first day I walked into class. The teacher didn't introduce me to the class. She looked back over her shoulder to see who walked in, then turned back and continued writing on the blackboard. I found an empty desk, sat down, and tried to figure out my surroundings.

In my new school, the cool Mexican girls told me I was trying to be white because it was a white thing to be studious. I also discovered that they differentiated between Mexican Americans and Mexicans from Mexico.

The "trendy" clothes my Mom had bought me with so much sacrifice back in Calexico were not the style in this new place. I started getting bullied by the older girls. It seemed that the thing to do was to be a bully myself. Cheerleading and soccer weren't "a thing" here. I arrived too late to join many of the school activities.

I was mocked for speaking with a Mexican accent. When trying to speak, I began to stutter, which had never been a problem before. Consequently, I became self-conscious and afraid to speak. Once again, the rules had changed, and I didn't understand the new rules.

My 1st Dress.

My self-esteem was nonexistent at this point, but I was happy that our aunts, uncles, and grandmother lived in L.A. That made handling this strange place with a completely new and intimidating culture a little more bearable.

I was growing up, and at the same time, we were trying to assimilate into a whole new culture. Many of the more mature girls wore pretty dresses, so I decided I would do the same. My friend gave me a jean dress, "Perfect," I thought. "I can wear it to our family gathering." They always dressed up, and I knew they'd be pleased that I'd finally done the same.

I carefully fixed my hair, applied lip gloss, and put on my crisply pressed denim dress. When it was time to go, I came out of my room looking self-conscious. Mom and my siblings looked at me with amusement, and I avoided their eyes. They'd never seen me in a dress as a teenager. Thankfully, no one mentioned it, which I completely appreciated.

I was very nervous. We drove to our family's house. From the looks of the parked cars outside, we were amongst the last to arrive. My siblings and I got out of the car, and Dad and Mom went and parked. We rang the doorbell, and a relative answered just as our parents were walking into their front gate.

The relative looked at me up and down, then opened the door wide so those inside could see me. She began to mock my dress loudly, "1st time you've worn a dress, and you chose that ridiculous dress?" "That dress looks like a rag; it is so ugly!" All the activity in the house stopped. All eyes were on me. My family, still on the porch waiting to come in, looked at me also, yet no one defended me.

I was utterly humiliated beyond words. It took all I had to get the nerve to wear a dress, and this scenario destroyed me. I walked into the house with my head down and sat in a corner, trying to disappear into the background so no one would notice my dress. I couldn't wait to leave so that I could take it off.

I was having a hard time adjusting and began to get angry. School wasn't the fun place that it had always been. I had one friend who was also new to the neighborhood; she was Filipino. She and her family lived in a beautiful home a few blocks away. Every day, we met on the corner and then walked together the rest of the way to school in the mornings.

One Friday morning, she asked me, "Hey, you want to go to a party tonight? It's at my friend's house."

The punch parties with parental supervision that I was used to came to mind. "I don't know, you have to ask my Dad," I said.

"Okay, I'll ask him."

After school, she said, "I'll be by later."

"Okay, see you later," I answered, unsure my Dad would even agree to let me go.

It started getting late. To my mind, parties finished around 10:00 p.m., so I figured she had changed her mind, but no, she came by around 7 p.m. I walked her into the living room.

"Dad," I said nervously. "My friend wants to ask you something."

"Hello, Mr. Quintero," my friend said cheerfully. "I was wondering if you would let Maria go with me to a party at my friend's house?" My dad didn't answer; he looked at us and turned back to watch his program. My friend and I waited in awkward silence.

"Who else is going to be there?" He finally asked, still not looking at us. "Will there be adult supervision?" He peppered her with questions. When she had answered his questions to his satisfaction, he finally agreed to let me go, with a caution, "You'd better behave." He said, looking straight at me.

I was in disbelief and overjoyed. "Oh man, what should I wear?" She was wearing eyelashes and was dressed simply. I had some flair: maroon corduroy pants, a simple quarter sleeve striped blouse, some flat, black, Mary Jane style shoes, and I wore a barrette in my hair. "Is this okay?" I asked after every clothing choice I made.

"Yeah, sure," she said nonchalantly without even looking.

Then we were off. We walked, giggling excitedly, down the long driveway towards the street, where a very nice car awaited. Her friend was behind the wheel. He looked full-grown; I thought he was "the adult supervision." I later found out he was actually her boyfriend! We got on the freeway, "I thought the party was close by?" I asked.

"Naw, it's up in the Hollywood Hills," she laughed. At the same time, she started changing in the car into a very revealing, fancy sequence top she had pulled out of her purse. She removed her flat shoes and slipped into some very high platform heels. "You want some?" She asked me as she looked in the rearview mirror and applied dark red lipstick. I don't think I even answered. She added more eye shadow and teased her hair up, adding hairspray. I was in the back seat watching all this go down. Her talent amazed me. I may have even had my mouth open; she had obviously done this before.

We arrived at a beautiful home on a large property as we drove around the curve on the top of the hill. The lawn was perfectly manicured, lighted flowerbeds and palms, and long wide steps going up to the house gave the whole front of the house an elegant flair.

We entered through the double doors. Other girls there dressed to the 9s, the same as my friend. All the guys looked older. I was definitely underdressed; I felt awkward. These were the days of Disco dancing, Soul Train lines, and American Bandstand. Girls wore high-platform shoes, but so did the guys. "These people are fancy," I thought.

Drinks flowed freely, the Disco music pumping and someone shouted, "Do The Hustle!" An enthusiastic group stood to their feet and rushed to the dance floor. Bumping me to the sofa in their excitement to dance. I watched them all dancing back and forth, stepping in unison. "Wow, so cool." I didn't know how to do the hustle.

As the night progressed, guys and girls were coupling off, and there was no parental supervision. I was sitting on the sofa when a guy asked me to dance. We danced a few times, and eventually, he tried to kiss me. Caught off guard, I said, "Hey!" and pushed him away. This made me uncomfortable and restless, and I could not wait to leave.

My friend was drunk, and she and her boyfriend were nowhere to be found. It was getting late, and I knew I'd be in trouble. Suddenly, my friend and her boyfriend appeared out of nowhere.

"When are we leaving?" I asked.

"Not for a while. It's a party, so party!" she said, lifting her drink.

"I have to call my Dad."

"Call him and just ask him if you can spend the night at my house."

I went to a quiet room with a house phone and called, "Dad? Can I spend the night at my friend's house?" He got the impression that we were already at her place, so he said, "Yes, but come home early." I felt terrible deceiving him.

I was uneasy. I didn't drink, so I got the full sober effect of what was happening around me. As the evening wore on, the beautiful girls were not so attractive anymore, and the guys were not as polite. Some couples disappeared into the expansive home, and I could only guess what was going on. A girl bumped into me hard, "Sorry!" she was walking her friend to the restroom to vomit.

I just wanted to go home, but my friend was not having it. Eventually, as the morning dawned, my friend was ready to go home. Her boyfriend was helping her walk, or he was leaning on her in order not to fall. I wasn't sure which. "Is he able to drive?" I asked. He was sure going to try. We swerved and braked awkwardly but finally got to my friend's house. Everyone in her home was asleep, and no one questioned her. We went straight to her room.

"We had such a great time last night at the party," she'd tell everyone who would listen when we were back at school. She then looked to me for confirmation.

"Yeah, we did," I said weakly, wondering if we had been at the same party.

"We have all become like one who is unclean, and all our righteous deeds are like a polluted garment. We all fade like a leaf, and our iniquities, like the wind, take us away." Isaiah 64:6 ESV

Chapter 15
Your Blouse is Inappropriate

I started making friends. I noticed others were including me and was even surprised to be voted as one of two "Princesses," and an 8th grader was voted queen to represent our school. We were going to ride a float for a Cinco De Mayo city parade. I was excited and felt that I was finally being accepted and fitting in.

Our family barely made ends meet, and the needs of growing kids made it difficult to provide luxuries. Mom had a favorite laundromat, and while the clothes washed, I would browse at Woolworths.

On this day, Mom said, "You can pick something from the $5 discounted rack." This made browsing more pleasant. I looked through the racks until I found a pretty T-shirt with some writing.

Neither I nor my Mom understood what the writing meant. We shrugged it off. I was just happy that the blouse was pretty, my size. The color was nice, and best of all, it was new! She purchased it, and I began thinking about how I could style it to wear the next day to school. I combed my hair in a slightly different way and put on a bit of lipstick one of my beautiful aunts had given me. I put my blouse on and went to school feeling a little classy. I got compliments throughout the day at school. I usually felt wrong and self-conscious, but not today. Today, I felt light and carefree as I went through the day.

After lunch, the school intercom sounded, "Maria Quintero to the Office, Maria Quintero to the Office." I walked to the office, curious as to why I was called. Apparently, I was in trouble. My Dad was already there, sitting on a chair against the wall. He looked nervous. They ushered us into the principal's office, where two other faculty members joined us. They began speaking, and I felt as if I had been transported to an alternate reality. "I dressed too maturely and was a bad influence on other students?"

I sat there stunned as they went on and on about me. The blouse I wore said, "Expensive, but worth it." I had no malice; I was naive to such things, and I thought *the blouse* was "expensive but worth it." Neither I nor my mom knew that it could have a derogatory meaning. I sat next to Dad as he listened quietly to the principal and a teacher discuss what would be done about me. They had to save the other students. I had to be removed, and their solution was to move me up a grade so I would not influence my classmates.

They felt I had the grades to graduate with the 8th-grade class. I sat there with a knot in my throat, humiliated, fighting back tears. I watched my Dad nod his head as he listened agreeably. I wanted him to defend me! Why was no one asking me about my side? What did I do? I was filled with shame. I had had a great day, and now I felt dirty and low. I had no idea what I had done wrong. I didn't even understand what the blouse said until many years later!

That morning, I put on my new blouse and felt confident. Now, here I was, holding back tears, being told that I was "bad" and needed to be kept from the others. My Dad just nodded in agreement. Years as an immigrant laborer had trained him that he was not entitled to an opinion. He had to be agreeable and not make waves.

I was immediately moved up to 8th grade and had to pass all the "Presidential Tests" to graduate to high school. In three weeks, I had to learn what all the other students had learned throughout the year. I wasn't confident that I could do it. However, confident or not, three weeks of intense studying followed. I took the tests, and I passed easily.

I should have been happy; instead, I was mad at the world, and I felt my heart harden. Every time I remembered that day the Principal had called my Dad to the office, I became angry, and my face got hot.

My school counselor was a kind lady. I tried to smile as she announced the high school I would be promoting to. However, my smile was forced and never reached my eyes.

I found out that I missed the school district boundary line by one street. So, I wouldn't be attending the same high school that all the other eighth graders would be going to. Instead, I and two other girls who missed the boundary would go to one of the rowdiest high schools. I was filled with apprehension just thinking about it.

That school had a bad reputation. They'd had race riots the previous year and, as a deterrent, had become one of the first schools in the area to be fully fenced in. It was locked down with only one way in and one way out.

I knew no one graduating 8th grade except those two girls I had seen around. I felt defeated; I had just started getting to know my 7th-grade classmates. Now, I was going to High School with total strangers.

I realize now that moving me up a grade during the last three weeks of school was a terrible choice, a big mistake I was not equipped to handle. As a result, this started me on a trajectory of self-destruction that I nearly didn't survive. It was too much to adjust to. I had just come from that innocent small town, and now, within less than a year, I would be going to high school with some very grown students.

Watching injustice when no one ever makes it right is disheartening. But we have a just God that we will all answer to one day. Be encouraged; one day, all the wrongs will be made right! We must put our lives into his jurisdiction and choose to belong to Him. He takes care of what is His.

"He will wipe every tear from their eyes. There will be no more death, mourning, crying, or pain, for the old order of things has passed." Revelation 21:4 KJV

My first year of high school was rough, as expected. The only thing that gave me some favor was that I was someone's doppelgänger. Her almost exact copy. People would walk by me and say, "Hey, Carmen." At least five times a day. Thankfully, she was well-liked and a Senior. She heard about me and had to come meet me. This started me off on the right foot to make some friends, and some of the popular crowd soon started befriending me. A few guys would talk to me, but they seemed very nervous.

 Eventually, one guy from the football team caught my interest and became my "boyfriend," but I never saw him outside of school. He was handsome, studious, nice, and treated me well. Our relationship consisted of talking, holding hands, and having lunch together, and he'd walk me to class. I think he kissed me awkwardly a few times. He'd call me on the phone and one day walked me home. Poor guy didn't know I lived clear across town. Other than that, it was a good friendship; I wasn't really interested in having a "boyfriend."

 May had ended, and I had just turned fifteen; I was starting my sophomore year. One day, Dad announced, "I signed you and Vince up for Martial Arts." He had also signed up. However, we exercised for one hour before we did our Sparring and Martial Arts forms. Dad was not coordinated enough, and the jumping jacks were the worst. He was hilarious as he jumped and landed on squatted open legs. Then he clapped his hands in front of his face as if catching flies. Then he jumped and stood up straight, swung his arms, and released the flies, slapping the sides of his hips. These were not smooth movements. They were instead individual, choppy movements that made him appear as if he were performing a funky dance all by himself. Everyone in the room tried hard not to giggle.

Dad gave it his best effort, but one day, he simply quit. Vince and I continued the classes.

It became my passion, and I was getting pretty good at it. I made a whole new set of friends in my Dojo. A couple of the students also attended my high school. I was enjoying this community. The achievements and exercise fueled me. The pride of discovering what my body could accomplish if I disciplined myself and worked hard gave me self-confidence. We became tightly knit and loved competing in various tournaments together.

There was a private class given to elite students. They were 3rd-degree black belt and above. One day, our instructor couldn't be there, and one of his elite students took the class. I felt a dark presence around him when he walked into the class. He was very mysterious and quiet but had power and authority. He noticed I was having difficulty doing the splits all the way flat to the ground. He walked up to me and told me, "Close your eyes." He whispered some strange words and laid his hands on my head. "Breathe in." I felt a powerful force, yet at the same time, I felt relaxed. "Exhale slowly." He commanded, "Open your eyes." I opened them and was shocked that I was easily flat to the ground. He piqued my curiosity about meditation techniques, Eastern Mysticism, and anything New Age. Although I felt a darkness around him, I loved when he came to teach.

One day, while at practice, I caught the eye of an older guy. He didn't attend our Dojo but kept coming around pretty regularly. After a while, he let me know that he was interested in me. We started talking as friends, and eventually, he became my boyfriend. Girls in my school found out about him liking me, and

I was taken aback because they made such a fuss. "You are going out with him?" They asked with huge smiles.

"I guess he is popular," I thought. Well, it turns out he was a big deal, and even though I had just started my Sophomore year, I found myself hanging out with the older crowd. Some of whom were still in high school. However, others were out of school already. This more mature crowd was involved in things that were way over my head. So, very quickly, I went from that small, innocent town punch and chip parties with parental chaperones to hanging out with this older crowd that drank, had sex, and used drugs. Teenagers aren't known for making the wisest decisions, and I certainly was not going to be any different.

The devil had waited years for the perfect setup, and naively, I walked right into it. Not realizing the ramifications of what I was walking into. He was Eighteen, and I had just turned fifteen.

"Hold on to instruction; do not let it go; guard it well, for it is your life. 14 Do not set foot on the path of the wicked or walk in the way of evildoers. 15 Avoid it, do not travel on it; turn from it and go on your way." Proverbs 4:13-15 NIV

Chapter 16
My First Real Date

    I waited with the joyful expectancy of the new. I was coming of age, and this was my first real boyfriend. Butterflies of first love filled me with anticipation. Was everything right? I didn't wear much makeup, just mascara and a little lip gloss. Was that okay? Did I choose the right blouse? I picked dark hunter green because I felt more mature wearing it. Form-fitting, but not revealing in any way. What does one do on dates? How does one behave? Do I need my own money?

    We had been hanging out for about six months, mainly with his family or friends. But we were never by ourselves, so a date was something new, something grown up. "He was picking me up for a date," I repeated for the umpteenth time. I liked the sound of that. Of course, my friends all knew because I had told them. He was well-liked and popular across all the social groups, and I noticed he was highly respected.

    My friends gushed, "He is so handsome, girl, you are lucky!" They were excited for me. New social doors opened because I was with him.

He picked me up in a cool muscle car, bright orange with a stripe running down the center from front to back.

He got off and opened the door for me; I smelled cologne. Getting in, I spotted his best friend in the back seat. I was seated in the front. I felt honored. My boyfriend introduced us. "This is Maria, Maria, this is Steven."

I overheard him ask his friend, "Guess how old she is?" He then added with a smirk, "She is just fifteen, jail bait."

I felt flattered that this handsome, popular guy would be interested in me. Suddenly, I was able to hang out with the in crowd. I felt accepted. Our family had moved so much that I was always the new girl, the outsider. Acceptance was something that I craved since childhood. It all felt so right.

House party.

We parked in a middle-class neighborhood; the street was packed with cars. We exited the vehicle, headed towards the house, and walked to the backyard of a home where everyone was gathered. He looked me in the eyes, smiled, held my hand, and we walked in. He introduced me to the adults and those in attendance as his girlfriend. I could tell these people were close to him and very fond of him.

They were all very kind and welcoming. The lady of the house greeted us with, "Finally, we meet her!" She then turned to me and shook my hand. "We've been hearing a lot about you," she said, smiling at my boyfriend.

We made a good couple, I thought. I felt valued and was ready to enjoy this new adventure with these new acquaintances. My life was coming together, and I loved how it was shaping up.

Music played from a stereo, and a few couples danced, but mostly, it seemed like a family gathering. The lady of the house pointed towards some kitchen chairs set up in a semicircle in the yard. I nodded and sat in one.

She came back with an 8oz glass of tequila with lemon and handed it to me. I had never had hard liquor before. I had a beer once before on the day I turned 15. I tried to have a second one, but my Mom put a stop to it quickly. I was with family then, surrounded by their watchful eye.

I wanted to fit in at this party and with this group of people, to be perceived as mature. As the woman next to me and I talked, I proceeded to drink the entire glass of tequila. The lady of the house noticed my empty glass and offered me more. "Isn't this what grown folk do?" I didn't know, so I said, "Yes, sure," to the second glass.

The sun went down while I was having a conversation with the woman who sat next to me. Except for a few lights here and there, I suddenly noticed that my surroundings became dark, "We've been chatting for a long while," I thought.

My boyfriend had been hanging out with the men the entire time, talking, laughing, and drinking. Once in a while, he glanced my way and smiled at me. I thought he was proud that I was making a good impression on these people who were obviously important to him.

After a while, he came to get me. I didn't feel the effect of the tequila until I tried to stand. I became dizzy as the tequila hit me like a violent ocean wave. He had to support me, but even then, I would flop to one side or the other, making it hard for him to walk me where he was trying to lead me.

He took me to the side of the house where there were no lights. It was isolated and dark. I had to adjust my eyes to see. I felt that the information coming to my mind was failing to register. I was confused about what was happening. It was coming to me slowly and in a jumbled form. I strained to make sense of things and of my surroundings. Everything was happening too fast.

He flopped me down onto an old sofa. I was dropped hard, and the couch seemed to have lost all its cushions. The situation was completely unexpected. I felt underwater, sluggish, and uncoordinated. I could not make any decisions or even judgments about what was occurring. I couldn't think clearly.

I do remember pulling away from him. I had believed I was safe with him. It slowly started dawning on my inebriated mind that I was not safe.

He was telling me something, ordering me around. He was not kind. He became forceful and threatening. I vaguely remember the feeling that someone was watching from behind a window—a teenage kid. Years later, when I allowed myself to think about this incident, I sensed he had done this to someone else before. I felt like the young kid knew this was going to happen when he saw him walking me to the side of the house in the dark.

That day, the day I felt so accepted. The day this handsome, popular guy walked proudly with me and made me feel beautiful. The day he introduced me with dignity to his inner circle—that day. The first day I drank tequila. I was a virgin… and I was date raped.

Everything was a blur after this. He later dropped me off at home. I entered a dark house; everyone was asleep. There was a fold-a-bed set up in the living room. For some reason, that was where I was sleeping at the time, but I don't remember why. I sat on my bed in the dark, scared, alone, and in severe pain. I was now sober; the feeling of anguish overwhelmed and terrified me. I knew sex was such a sacred thing, reserved for marriage. The women in my family prided themselves on reaching marriage while still virgins. That had been my goal as well. Now, here I was, sick to my stomach; I didn't understand what had happened.

I knew I had lost something precious; I felt stupid and dirty. I was sure it was my fault. I told no one what happened.

"It is better to take refuge in the Lord than to trust in man." Psalms 118:8 NIV

I had been raised with strong morals. Not proud, not looking down nor judging others, just knowing what is right and wrong. When I hung out with friends, I was careful to draw my boundaries, trying to do right. I had been taught that there were boundaries you just did not cross. I had seen my aunts and other family members guard their purity and had every intent to be a virgin when I walked down the aisle. I believed it to be a beautiful gift to give the man I would marry.

The order of things deeply ingrained in me had been broken. I had a road map to follow. I had gone off course and now didn't know how to proceed. I felt broken beyond repair. I was filled with deep sadness and apprehension, heartbroken. I felt devastated, ruined, and filthy; no decent man would ever want me.

"How do I face him?" My mind was malfunctioning. The thought of my boyfriend hurting me in a heartless way was not computing. My heart was shattered; I felt it physically shatter.

"Oh God, don't let my parents ever find out!"

The thought of "tomorrow" terrified me. I couldn't sleep. Inevitably, night turns into day, and I could not stop tomorrow from coming.

"Maybe it was just a nightmare?" I thought as I slowly awoke. As I tried to get up, I felt pain and realized it was all true. My groggy mind cleared, and I felt a wave of panic. What had happened the night before was wrong at so many levels. First, an almost nineteen-year-old had sex with a barely fifteen-year-old virgin, whom an adult had served an excessive amount of alcohol, then had been sexually violated on their property. These were crimes, but my mind could not allow me to face that fact. This horrible reality was too much for me to handle. I went into denial.

My coping mechanism of choice was to change the reality of what had happened to me. I created a new reality in my head. "I was just dumb; I had gotten drunk and chose to have sex." It was easier to think this because then the rejection and victimization were not as severe or painful. I could not bear to think that I had been victimized by someone I loved and trusted.

This way, I could hold on to my delusion that I was cared for, loved, and had found my forever boyfriend.

I continued to see my boyfriend, pretending that nothing had happened. I was determined to go on with life as usual, determined to go on with high school.

Little did I know that trauma cannot be ignored. Nor could it be swept under the carpet. No matter how hard you try to push it down, It is like a giant beach ball you keep trying to push underwater. Eventually, it will pop up somewhere, and you may not be able to control how it manifests.

"The Lord is close to the brokenhearted and saves those who are crushed in spirit." Psalm 34:18 NIV

Chapter 17
He Tried to Kidnap Me

My boyfriend bragged to his close friend, who was even older than he (in his late 20s), that he'd had sex with me. He didn't realize it, but his friend was a sex predator and began to call me. He could sense I was naive; he sensed my shame. "What will your parents do if they find out what you did?" "If you tell anyone I'm calling you, I will tell everyone what you did."

He read me and knew I was terrified of others finding out about what had happened. His friend began to blackmail me. I feared him, and I wasn't ignorant to the fact that he was trying to coerce me to meet him somewhere and intended to then assault me. I became paranoid. I would not walk by myself anywhere, not even in the daytime.

One evening, I went to our apartment carport to get something I'd left in the car. Suddenly, someone wrapped their arms around me from behind violently.

I was completely taken aback, and my mind couldn't grasp what was happening. I was home in my safe space. Who was this? What did they want?

It was this predator that had been threatening me on the phone. He was a large man. My head came to his chest, and he caught me completely by surprise.

I pushed him away with all my might, but he was too strong for me. I smelled the reeking of alcohol in his breath and his clothing. "Leave me alone; let go of me." I kept pushing, squirming, trying to escape his tight bear hug, but I couldn't even loosen his hold. My feet left the ground as he pulled me towards his parked car. Fear gripped me at the realization that I was not getting away.

Suddenly, someone came from around the corner and startled him. He loosened his hold, and I was able to drop all my weight and slip down out of his grip.

"What's going on?" It was my Dad; he was getting his car to go to his night job. As he turned the corner, he was suddenly confronted with some guy holding me in the dark.

He didn't realize I needed help. Instead, he assumed I was a willing participant. He didn't see the fear in my eyes. He simply gave me a dirty look and got in his car. My heart pounding hard, I ran back into our apartment.

The predator was caught off guard, too confused to do anything, and I didn't stick around to see what he would do.

He had found my home! How long had he been out there waiting for me? He was daring and tried to assault me right in front of my apartment! I knew I had narrowly escaped being raped, kidnapped, and who knows what this evil man had planned. I went to the window and saw he was still out there!

Again, I told no one. I felt fear of this man. More than anything, the deeper wound I felt was that my Dad thought I was willingly sneaking around with this monster! As he got in his car, he turned to look at me. I felt his accusing eyes pierce my heart. How could he think this of me? I cried as I thought of his disappointed look and how he had just gotten in his car and drove away—not knowing if I was okay or not.

After this incident, I began to lose my resolve to be "good." Anger began to grow. I thought, "If that is what my Dad thinks of me, then that is what I will be."

It's like hoping for rain amid a drought, searching for rain clouds in a bright, sunny sky.

I was losing my grip on hope.

"Finally, the seventh time, his servant told him, "I saw a little cloud about the size of a man's hand rising from the sea." Then Elijah shouted, "Hurry to Ahab and tell him, 'Climb into your chariot and go back home. If you don't hurry, the rain will stop you!'"

1 Kings 18:44 NLT

Sometimes hope is small; it can barely be mustered up, and this causes us to wonder, "What can such small hope do against this overwhelming situation?" Never underestimate hope. When God is who our hope is based on, that small cloud can bring an abundance of rain!

We hope to be fully known. We also hope that when others accuse us of something contrary to our character, someone will rise and say, "No! I know them, they wouldn't do that, that's not who they are!"

We hope those who know us and claim to believe in us will defend our integrity. If any accusation is ever made against us, they would rise to our defense.

It hurts deeply when someone with whom you've done life, someone to whom you have repeatedly proven yourself, believes the worst of you.

It occurred to me that day that not only was my Dad doubting my honor, but he was also thinking the worst of me. This devastated me. I loved my Dad, and it was important that he be proud of me.

However, I was doing the same to God. The God that I grew up believing in. The God I had learned to trust in and honor. I was now seeing him as cruel, indifferent, and non-caring. My heart was beginning to accuse him. I was becoming stony.

Trauma Will Distort Reality

I just recently became aware that in telling the story of the date rape and all the terrible consequences that followed, I tend to underestimate its negative effect on me even today. This event was the catalyst for the horrible downward spiral that followed.

I did not want to have premarital sex with my boyfriend. I had a conviction that it was wrong. I still didn't realize how badly traumatized I was. At this point, I was just trying to survive.

I thought, "Maybe if I tell him I'm pregnant, he'll leave me alone and not try to be with me." I believed somehow, I could make this relationship work. I wasn't pregnant but knew very little about sex, so I thought this would keep him away from me.

I kept trying to figure out a way to escape from my sad reality. I hoped I was wrong and that he really did love me and was sorry for hurting me. I deeply wished to return things to how they were before that evening when sex was forced on my incoherent, drunk body.

Getting away from this guy and breaking off this toxic relationship didn't occur to me. Somehow, in my 15-year-old mind, I thought this relationship was salvageable. Or maybe I had the old-school mentality of, "Now you have to stay with him." I was an ignorant little girl who was not street-smart and over her head!

I thought, what if it gets back to him that I'm not pregnant? So I pretended I was with everyone. But when I thought of that night, I felt embarrassed, ashamed, and remorseful. I felt stupid. I wanted to blurt out what happened to me, but it wouldn't come out. I felt the pressure of the beach ball (trauma) that I was trying so hard to keep submerged.

I wanted to tell someone, but my mouth wouldn't open. I just remained silent. What baffles me to this day is that I'd continue to see my boyfriend. This was the depth of my denial.

I have since learned that many victims do just that, though. They go into denial and blame themselves. A significant percentage of victims stay with their abuser.

So I stayed with him. However, the shine was gone. The beauty of this relationship was gone. All I felt was disappointment, apprehension, and desperation to change the narrative of reality. I felt lost.

I realized that my boyfriend didn't really care about me. I was not the girlfriend he was hoping for. Someone who would just "live that party life " with him. He wasn't happy that sex wasn't going to become a part of our relationship, so we fought constantly. I wasn't going to be that girlfriend who hung out in a constant cloud of drugs, crime, and parties.

I was filled with wariness as I slowly began to discover that he had long ago gone deep into the pit he was now trying to pull me into.

Slowly, the reality of what was going on began to dawn on me. I heard rumors of drugs regularly. He and his friends would go into another room for a while. Although I didn't know it then, they were injecting heroin, the drug of choice of that era.

I heard conversations about drive-bys, and I saw his guns. Not many of his friends worked regular jobs. Prison sentences were worn like a badge of honor. Homeboys who "got out" were treated like returning war heroes. I was a little confused by their values.

One day, he and his friend were sitting in his front yard laughing; I overheard them talking about having just stabbed someone. This freaked me out. "He is a bad person!"

I began to see his "normal," and I was very conflicted. Although I loved him, I did not want this kind of life. I saw how things turned out for some of the girls that lived that life.

I witnessed his friend's girlfriends getting high right along with their boyfriends. Some were slapped around and cussed at regularly. When their boyfriends were unfaithful, they looked for the girl and gave her a beat down, but the guys got off scot-free. The guys felt proud of their girls for fighting for them.

Some of them were pregnant and had to go on welfare. Some were getting strung out. Guys no longer wanted them when they lost their beauty and self-respect. Crime was normal, and I saw the evil around me. I sensed the dead-end, but I was ignorant of the depth of the darkness trying to entrap me. I felt like I was on the edge of a spewing volcano, teetering and about to fall in. I was determined not to allow myself to be torn down.

Depression is our soul reaching its breaking point. It's our heart telling us that it has been suffering for far too long. It has been traumatized by the prolonged experience.

We've been wounded and in need of care, but no one has taken the time to heal us.

In desperation, our body begins to tell on us. Uncovering the secrets we hide. It cries out for help. It either shuts down and refuses to function or experiences full-on trauma symptoms. It fights hard for survival without our permission or cooperation.

I became depressed but didn't know it. All I knew was that my life had lost all its beauty. I remember going for days, hardly speaking. Everything felt soiled. I could sit staring at the wall for hours in the middle of a chore, deep in thought yet unsure what I had been thinking about. I dwelt in the shadows as my dreams slipped out of my hands.

I felt disillusioned and confused, but that just made me double up in my determination that nothing would break me. I was not going to go down. I refused to become a statistic; but I was fighting alone, and I'm sure often, I was simply beating the air. I was fighting a losing battle.

"Trust in the Lord with all your heart and lean not on your own understanding; 6 in all your ways submit to him, and he will make your path straight. 7 Do not be wise in your own eyes; fear the Lord and shun evil." Prov. 3:5-7 NIV

Chapter 18

If Tomorrow Starts Without Me

If your heart is broken and you are in anguish, don't make a permanent decision in your temporary pain! Hang on, you will come out of this! ...God has not left you!

I know this now, but I didn't realize then that God can be trusted. I didn't know he cared; I thought he was distant and indifferent. I believed we were on our own; it was up to us to fix our mess. Even as life overwhelms us, God is calling us. We don't have to do it alone.

Strange enough, although I was unaware of God's love for me, I was aware of darkness and evil. I felt it. I saw it; I could sense it. Evil is an entity driven by its hate for us; it delights in our pain.

You see, my obituary was supposed to read:

Maria Luz Quintero, born in 1961, Died in 1976 at the young age of 15. Survived by a heartbroken Mother and father, four devastated siblings, two brothers and two sisters. She never graduated, was never married, never had children. She never realized how much she was loved by her family but most of all by a beautiful God who had been actively pursuing her since she was a child.

At the beginning of this book, I told of being controlled by an evil entity that directed me to commit suicide by taking many, many pills.

I have no clear memory of anything else from the point that I went to bed with all those drugs in my system. If Satan had his way, I was living my last hours.

I'm sure hell was frenzied with excitement at the thought of another soul being lost. Taken to an eternal torment without the knowledge of salvation - salvation afforded freely by a generous Savior who had loved me. He gave himself for me so I would not have to find myself in this hopeless position.

No one ever told me, though. I had taken these pills under the power of an evil stronger than me. I was no match to resist it or fight it. Although unconscious, I have spotty memories of lying on a hospital bed.

Later on in life, many years later, I began thinking about the day I took the pills. "How did my sisters know something was wrong with me? How did they know that I was overdosing?"

Everyone had gone to bed, and I was meant to slip into eternity without anyone even realizing it. They were supposed to sleep through the night, only to find my lifeless body in the morning. What a cruel thing to do to my family!

But as I said before, something was controlling me and instructing me every step of the way. I was unable to resist this entity. I was not even able to think of resisting. It was a done deal. Somehow, this thing had the right to me and to control me completely. It instructed, and I obeyed.

I had never really allowed myself to remember and acknowledge those events fully.

Something else that I hadn't allowed myself to think about was the fact that my family experienced the full trauma of my attempting suicide. I had not looked at it from their point of view before. I wondered what their experience had been. This caused me to ask my sisters what they experienced that evening.

It was painful hearing the following, but it was necessary. My sisters Norma and Martha's combined account; "Our youngest sister, Norma, and I were sleeping, and a gurgling sound woke us up. It was you. We tried to wake you up, but you wouldn't't wake up. You got up, but you looked more like a rag doll being lifted by your collar, like dead weight. Then suddenly, you were dropped. Your head hit the corner of the dresser. You hit hard on your temple, which caused you to vomit a bit. You opened your eyes and stared at us. Your eyes were red, bloodshot, and evil. You looked at us with hate and lunged at us like you wanted to hurt us. We ran to our parent's bedroom to get our Mom and Dad.

We woke them up, and they rushed to the room. They saw you. Your mascara was running down your face, your eyes were red, and you had vomited a bit. It smelled like medication, so Dad told us to run and get the paramedics. (We lived right across the street from the Fire Station.)

The rocks hurt my feet as I ran down the long driveway barefooted. I ran across the four-lane highway to the corner Fire Station. Norma was with me; we knocked on their door repeatedly. It was still night-time, so they were asleep. It seemed like a long time, but finally, one paramedic answered the door. He grabbed his first aid bag and followed me home. Then the rest came in the fire truck.

They walked into our room, checked you, and tried to determine what they smelled. They asked if there was an empty pill bottle somewhere. Your hitting your head had knocked the pill bottles and the note behind the dresser. They couldn't find them. From experience, they identified the pills by the smell. They administered first aid as we all stood by and watched. We were scared. The paramedics put your semi-conscious body on a gurney and rushed you to the hospital."

My terrified parents feared their daughter was dying. Was I going to be gone when they reached the hospital? They quickly dressed and followed the ambulance in disbelief and despair. Everyone was sending up private prayers, "God help her."

Norma says, "Next thing I knew, we were visiting you at the hospital. Your friends were also there, so we didn't't get too much time with you, so we came back home and waited, hoping you would return.

Will she live or die?

When the medical team first tried to treat me, I was cussing and violent, pulling out whatever tubes I was connected to. They inserted a tube down my throat and pumped the remaining pills out of my stomach, but my body had already absorbed much of the pills. Eventually, I fell into a coma.

I was unconscious, but I vaguely remember lying in the hospital bed. Although I had my eyes shut, I heard some of what went on but could not communicate.

I can remember voices I recognized, friends, and family. Some comforted my mom, who sat beside my bed praying, pleading with God that he would spare my life. "You can have her God, but please not like this. Spare her life, God. Please don't take her like this."

I, however, felt disconnected from what was going on. I had no feelings or cognitive thoughts. I was an uninvolved spectator. I was not aware of the seriousness of what had happened. I didn't feel regret for what I had done because, in all reality, I hadn't done it. Something took control of me. I didn't think of death, nor did I feel empathy for the suffering I had caused. I wasn't alarmed or worried about why I was in this hospital. I still didn't have complete control of my will. I still felt highjacked, hypnotized.

"But as for me, my feet had almost slipped; I had nearly lost my foothold." Psalm 73:2 NIV

Chapter 19

The Near Death Experience (NDE)

I didn't know what day it was or how long I had been lying in the hospital. I had no sense of time, but suddenly, I felt my soul lifting, separating from my body. I found myself gliding through an arid landscape. I wasn't walking, nor was I flying. It felt like gliding about as fast as riding a bike full speed at a height of about 12 feet.

I saw a desert all around. I don't recall many details about the passing bare, arid terrain, but I remember seeing hills on either side. It went by quickly. Then a Raintree came into view. The full, green foliage formed a dome at the top.

Next, my eyes focused on a huge brown bolder next to the tree. I then began to see a figure wearing turquoise blue. I realized it was a beautiful woman with dark black curls. Wearing a long blue chiffon nightgown with a matching turquoise blue chiffon overcoat in the 1950s style. It moved in the wind, reminding me of a waterfall.

Involuntarily, I slowed down and stopped. It was more like a landing. This was my destination.

The woman approached me in a friendly and familiar way; she didn't seem to think it strange that I was there; it was as if I were expected. She chatted with me as if we were simply visiting over coffee. "I'm your Aunt Maggie," she said with a huge smile. It was a very relaxed conversation, an effortless exchange.

  We sat at a small table. It felt like a scene in the theatre. All that was in focus was the small area surrounding the tree and boulder. Everything else was dark and out of focus, like when you are watching a play on the theater stage and you only see what is under the spotlight. I did have a sense that just in the shadows, nearby, was an entity I didn't see nor hear, but I felt was there.

  She was beautiful and easy to talk to, and soon, we were deep in conversation. The specifics are fuzzy. I had her full attention, and she was genuinely interested in me and what I had to say. We laughed a lot; she got my humor. What a pleasant visit!

  Then suddenly, it was as though there was an unseen authority she was submitting to. She had limits and parameters she had to abide by, and she knew I had to leave. We didn't discuss it; without notice, I lifted and then found myself gliding in reverse through the desert. Then suddenly, I was back in my body again, in my hospital bed, still unable to communicate or respond to my family.

  I was vaguely aware of what was happening in the room. I wasn't catching everything because it all felt hazy and very distant. However, some of the voices were familiar. There were moments of silence when the gloomy atmosphere seemed to thicken. People were there to visit me, to comfort my family, and I believe I smelled flowers at one point.

I heard a particular voice; it was a friend who, at one time, walked with the Lord. He never said so; however, I now know that his speech betrayed him. The language he used and the truths he knew I now recognize as Christian "faith talk." He was running from Truth, but it would slip out of his mouth in conversation.

He had become an alcoholic and drug user. I was hanging out with him before the suicide attempt overdose. He never let me see him taking drugs, but I had learned to recognize the signs. He was very respectful and always looked out for me.

He once picked me up in his chopper, and I could tell he'd been drinking. I was concerned and questioned his ability to drive. The chopper stalled, and he kept trying to kick start it. After multiple attempts, he sat on the grass in defeat, completely drenched in sweat. He had sweated out the alcohol and sobered up. Sitting on the curb, he shook his head and said, "Man, I need to get myself right; I'm tired!" I didn't know about the Lord back then, so I thought he meant he needed to get sober.

But He was a "backslider". Someone who had been saved, known the Lord, and walked away. He left the Lord in exchange for the "pleasures of sin." It doesn't last; eventually, payday comes, and the devil leaves you empty, miserable, and often addicted to some bondage.

"Choosing rather to suffer affliction with the people of God than to enjoy the pleasures of sin for a season." Hebrews 11:25 KJV

He had known how broken, miserable, and lost I felt, yet he didn't tell me about the Savior who could rescue me. Now, he was here at my deathbed. As he spoke to my Mom, I heard regret and fear in his voice. Fear that he could have shared hope, salvation, and deliverance with me, but he never did.

He now communicated Bible truths with her. Lying there in that hospital bed, what I overheard didn't reach me. There was no power behind his words; his life contradicted the truth he knew. I could have used this truth, I was a captive, a prisoner to an evil entity. I needed a Savior. Still, I believe he contacted his friends and family, who were believers and walking with the Lord and asked them to pray for me. Possessing the truth of The Gospel when one finds oneself in situations that are way out of our realm of understanding gives us something to hold on to. The light shines through the darkness, and even in this land between death and life, the gospel we know is a powerful defense in our arsenal. The Gospel provides us with truth to make the right choice to repent and turn to Jesus while we still have the choice. I could have used the truth with what happened next…

I suddenly lifted out of my body again and found myself gliding through the desert. This was involuntary, and it seemed that someone had the power to summon me. After a bit, the round Raintree came into focus. Under it, to the right, was the large brown boulder. Slowly, the turquoise blue shape came into focus, and my beautiful aunt Maggie greeted me with a smile. I was limited to that small area under the Raintree. I could go nowhere else and could see nothing else. Regardless, I felt such excitement. What a pleasant and nurturing person; I was elated about these visits!

Again, we laughed and smiled, talked and chatted about things. Then again, it was unspoken, but it was time for me to go. There was never a goodbye; it was just something that was known. I found myself gliding through light brown hills and beige arid desert terrain. Then I was back in the room in my hospital bed. I heard the din of activity. Sounds from medical machines and nurses' voices down the hallway—distant, vague conversations and activities taking place in my room. I was a spectator, not awake yet, still unable to communicate.

The out-of-body experiences happened numerous times, maybe three to four times. I'm not entirely sure how long the trips took in real-time or how far apart they occurred. I was completely disconnected from any sense of time. Two different realities were going on simultaneously. At the same time, my family was grief-stricken, hoping and praying, exhausted, and filled with worry. I was having these out-of-body experiences. I was unaware that what was happening to me was fearful, nor that I teetered between life and death and that I should be alarmed.

Nor was I aware I should be filled with regret and apprehension that I had put myself and my family in this serious condition. If someone had communicated the gospel to me prior to finding myself in this hospital bed, then I would have light and direction. I was not conscious, but I was still alive. The truth of the gospel would have given me an understanding that I was in danger and needed to make a choice. Repent and receive Christ and be ready for the next life. But no one had witnessed to me. I didn't have The Word in me. The Word of God that does not return unto Him (God) void, but goes out and accomplishes what it was sent out to do. I knew I still had the freedom of choice, even in the unconscious state, but I was defenseless.

Again, my soul separated from my body; I traveled to this place, and everything was as before. I had a lovely time with my Aunt Maggie. Towards the end of our time together, she said, "I like you; you are so funny!" Pleased to hear this, I answered, "I like you too. I love talking and visiting with you," I added.

"Do You? Then why don't you just come with me?" She said with a twinkle in her eye. I could not believe my ears; my beautiful Aunt was inviting me to go with her.

"I can?" I asked.

"Of course, you can," Aunt Maggie answered quickly, leaning in to punctuate her assertion.

"Yes, I'd love to!"

"Okay, next time you come, you will go with me. Now go, you have to leave," she said with a bit of urgency.

I was overjoyed at the thought of going with her. I glided through the now familiar desert; the scenery was familiar, and I found myself back in the hospital bed.

I couldn't care less what was going on in the room. I felt no compassion for my grieving mother, family, or friends who came to see me. I felt divorced from this life; I had absolutely no interest in it whatsoever. All I could think of was going with my

Aunt Maggie. I didn't even ask myself, "Where?" Where was she taking me? I was full of eager anticipation, waiting to leave my body again so I could finally "go" with her. Once again, where? Where was she so anxious to take me? I felt as if she had won a high-stakes game. I was ignorant, and an easy prey.

I don't know how much time passed or how long I had to wait. But soon enough, I once again found myself gliding. The desert came into view, the raintree, under it to the right, the huge brown boulder. I was giddy with excitement. I knew what came next: the long, blue chiffon nightgown, my aunt Maggie.

However, neither the blue gown nor my Aunt Maggie came into view. Instead, an older gentleman stood in the spot where she usually waited. I landed, a bit puzzled. Then, as I focused, it began to dawn on me that this gentleman looked like my grandfather Santiago (James).

He's wearing a brown beige khaki shirt, rolled-up sleeves, and matching pants. The shirt is tucked in, and he wears a worn brown leather belt.

"Grandpa!" I happily called out, but he wasn't happy to see me.

He does not smile. He says sternly, "What are you doing here?"

I say, "Grandpa, It's me." As I try to throw my arms around him (He was my favorite male figure, a hard-working man with a great sense of humor. In my eyes, he was a genius and made me feel safe.)

He evaded my hug, pulled away, and said sternly, "Don't touch me!"

I was hurt and heartbroken by his cold demeanor and rejection. "Grandpa, why are you treating me like this?" I asked fighting back tears. "You need to get out of here, you don't belong here, you need to leave NOW!" he answered.

I felt hurt and then angry. I replied, "NO! My Aunt Maggie asked me to go with her, and I am going with her!"

Once again, very sternly, he said. "Get out of here, you don't belong here."

I stubbornly answered, "My Aunt Maggie invited me to go with her, and I'm going with her!"

He looked me in the eyes without touching me and impatiently said, "DON'T YOU KNOW SHE'S DEAD!"

I gasped, felt a shock go through me like electricity, and instantly found myself on my bed in my hospital room. There was no lifting and gliding, no desert scenery. I was just instantly back in my body.

I woke up from the coma, very confused, uncertain, and panicking; what in the world happened?

"The cords of death entangled me, the anguish of the grave came over me; I was overcome by distress and sorrow." Psalm 116:3 NIV

Chapter 20

She made it through; she is awake!

The first thing my eyes focused on was my Dad standing before my gloomy hospital room's large window. He stood with his back to me, but his face turned slightly so that it was within my view. The window in the room allowed some sunlight in, and I could see his expression as he looked out into the busy city of Los Angeles. I heard him crying softly. I called out to him, "Dad?"

"You're awake! This is about the time you were born," he said as if that was what he had been thinking about. He just looked at me sadly, yet glad I was alive. "I would have never expected this from you. I always thought you were the strong one, Mija." He looked at me as if trying to figure out why I would try to end my life.

Then said suddenly, "Are you hungry?" I don't think I answered. He then told the nurses, "She's woken up, bring her some food."

How do I tell my Dad what I had just experienced? I was in a state of shock.

The other patients had already eaten dinner, and it was too early for breakfast, but the nurse walked in with a food tray for me. "I think it's mashed potatoes," my Dad said, adding salt to them. I just nodded, It turns out it was cream of wheat with milk and sugar, and now, thanks to my Dad, salt, plenty of salt. He began lovingly feeding me this disgusting bowl of salty, sweet cream of wheat. I didn't complain; I was still trying to figure out what had happened to me on those trips I had been taking. I was in a state of confusion, and I didn't have the language to communicate what I had just experienced.

The doctors came in later, and some tests followed to ensure there was no residual brain damage or any other lasting effect from the overdose. With all the tests and prodding, they could not, however, look into my shattered soul. There was plenty of damage there. Did anyone notice?

They deemed me healthy, so my parents were informed I would be released to go home.

But what happened to me? Can someone please explain? What was speaking to me and guiding me in such an intense, hypnotic way to end my life? Where did I go? What was that place? Who were these people I had visited with? Why did I visit with Aunt Maggie, and why did my Grandpa say she was dead? Why didn't he let me touch him?

No one brought up the suicide attempt. If the incident had to be referred to for any reason, they would say, "When that happened" or "What you did," but suicide was never mentioned.

No one asked, "Exactly what were you going through, and why would you take such a final way out?" But to be honest, if asked, I don't think I would have had any answers.

It's strange, but I can't say that the suicide attempt was something I did willingly. I don't know if I will be believed, but I was under the control of something else that had the power to manipulate me completely. So much so that it felt as though it had all happened to someone else.

Mom and Dad took me home. They gave me their double bed to rest on. This was a token of love from my parents. They purchased a pretty blue nightgown for me to relax in. Some family came to visit me. I was surrounded by the cards and flowers that family and friends had brought me.

Some family members showed sincere concern for me; from others, I sensed morbid curiosity to come and see "The girl who had tried to kill herself."

You Didn't Get Away, You Traitor!

It was good to be home; I was exhausted. I also felt like my hair had not been washed in weeks. My little sister was by my side "Will you help me wash my hair? I don't think I can do it alone."

"Sure," she said, looking at me, unsure of what to make of the whole "suicide, hospital stay" ordeal. We both went to the bathroom. I felt weak and was so grateful that she was willing to help me. I knelt with my head over the bathtub. She got a Tupperware tumbler to pour water on my hair. I shampooed my hair, and she rinsed it. Although I felt better, I also needed someone to help me make sense of what had happened to me. I didn't understand why I did such a terrible thing. Why did I try to kill myself? How did this thing take control of me, what was it, and will it do it again? I felt insecure and unsafe.

Everyone was gathered in the nice sunny living room, so I walked there feeling better with freshly washed hair and sat in our oversized orange recliner. The matching sofa had long ago been thrown out. However, we still owned the matching recliner. Exhausted, I began to dose off. People were milling around; I heard the buzz of conversation. I felt like I had run a marathon, so tired. Eventually, my eyes closed. However, I was alarmed by what happened next and was caught completely by surprise. As I dozed in and out, I again saw my aunt Maggie (the one I had been visiting in my Near Death Experience, back at the hospital.) It didn't feel like a dream; it felt like I SAW her.

She didn't look the same, nor did she sound the same, but I knew it was her. She looked down at me through what seemed like a dirty window, but she was no longer beautiful.

Her beautiful, dark curls now looked matted, disheveled, and dirty; her eyes were bloodshot red, and they had black running down like the guys on KISS (the heavy metal band). Her eyes were filled with utter hate for me, her lips were gone, and that part of her face had no skin and resembled a skeleton with filthy, dirty teeth!

She shrieked at me with utter hatred and rage, "You think you got away from me, you traitor!" I felt heat radiate from her. Adrenaline rushed to my brain, fear pulsed through me, and my body felt faint! I knew that I was in the presence of evil!

"You didn't get away; I am going to get you, you traitor!" she growled.

I woke with a violent start; I tried to jump out of the recliner and get away, feeling horror run through me. "My aunt Maggie wants to get me!!" I whimpered, terrified. Why is she pursuing me? Why is she calling me a traitor?" We still had company, but I wasn't censoring my words; I felt terrorized and didn't care who heard me.

I looked to those in the room pleading for help and caught a glimpse of my mom's eyes, filled with concern, unsure if I was just seeking attention. Mom seemed embarrassed for me, concerned that I was making a scene in front of the company. She feared that my visitors would tell others I was not okay. That I was either crazy or just seeking attention.

I didn't care; I was crying out for help. What was happening?

My Mom had pained eyes; she wondered what she could do to help me.

But this was real; It was happening to me! I did see the angry, evil demon that had posed as my aunt and tried to get me to agree to go with it!

Every time I started to doze off, this scene would be repeated; not only would I see her, but the atmosphere would become charged with dark, evil energy. I could physically feel the hate as she repeatedly growled, "I hate you, you traitor; you did not get away!" I was harassed.

To avoid seeing this demon, I tried extremely hard not to fall asleep, but exhaustion would eventually get the upper hand, and inevitably, I would doze off, and again, I'd see her. It didn't matter if it was daytime; it made no difference if I was surrounded by a room full of people. This demon showed up and terrorized me as soon as I began to doze off.

I cried out to those in the room, "My aunt Maggie wants to get me; she says she hates me, and she's gonna get me!". I was sleep-deprived and felt utterly defeated and in despair at realizing I was not being taken seriously.

The looks of pity I got from everyone told me that they thought I maybe had mental issues.

My mom seemed exasperated; she bent over and whispered so that no one could hear, "You need to stop saying that your aunt Maggie is going to get you, Maria. Her mom is here; that's her daughter. Please stop saying that."

A few days later, a visiting relative sat with me and asked me, "Why do you say that Aunt Maggie wants to get you?"

"Because she does!" I said, explaining how she presented herself as beautiful, but now her appearance was evil, like decaying flesh.

He looked around, assuring himself no one was listening, then in hushed tones, added, "Did you know that you had an Aunt Maggie?"

I thought I had heard of her when I was very little. "She died by suicide in the prime of her life," he added.

"No!, I hadn't known that!" This caught me off guard.

Wow, that information hit me hard! A realization of Satan's wicked strategy against me was brought to light. An evil scheme was exposed, a revelation of the modus operandi of evil. This same familiar demon that had convinced her to take her life had now also tried to take mine! It came to me as a beautiful, pleasant, loving, friendly "angel of light." It intended to take my life. I had no defense against this demon. I don't know how I knew this, but I did. I shuddered at the realization that It almost succeeded in killing me, too.

This same demon was now tormenting me when I tried to sleep. It was now showing its true nature and was furious because it failed at its assignment. I got away, or at least I thought I did.

No one else saw it; they thought I was either faking to get attention or, worse, that I had lost my mind and was now mentally unstable.

I didn't sleep for weeks; the demon was still tormenting me. My family became very concerned and desperate. They began to think maybe I wasn't okay mentally, so I was referred to the mental hospital. I had to speak to a psychiatrist. I went, and they prescribed medication, but it didn't help. Eventually, I realized that if I didn't want them to drug me or commit me to the mental hospital, I couldn't speak about my reality, what I saw, what I felt. So, I just told them what they wanted to hear. It worked, and eventually, I was told matter of factly, "We can no longer help you," and that I didn't't need to return.

Back at home, my Mom returned to work, and a few friends began to come by to check on me now and then. They brought alcohol or marijuana; I couldn't smoke because I became severely paranoid, but alcohol became my "salvation," or so I believed. I didn't realize alcohol had taken many of my family members down. It would solve nothing. I would soon find myself trapped. However, alcohol helped me get some sleep. I had no other solution; only then did I manage to ignore the apparitions, the visions, or whatever they were. I reasoned that only supernatural help could genuinely help me with the torment, so I looked into the supernatural. I listened to mediums on TV. My friend's older sister was a flower child and loved to teach us about finding our spirit guides and about the many Hindu gods we could pray to. My Martial Arts instructor would lead us in guided meditation. I longed for peace, so I was easy prey.

I also wanted my life back; I'd grown restless staying home and had to get back to school, back to society. Maybe even back to dreaming, pursuing, striving, and achieving goals, back to everyday life.

I didn't know it then, but my "normal" was gone; I had no paradigm to understand that the enemy had done his damage, the threats were real, and I hadn't completely gotten away.

I was ignorant of the fact that I had been systematically bound in chains. The entity that had caused me to overdose and attempt to kill myself was still there; no one had made it leave, and no one I knew could. Most didn't believe it was real; they thought it was all in my head. I didn't even realize that it was still there. I was a slave and severely demonized.

Chapter 21
Back in School

I returned to school but felt entirely out of place, out of the loop, and out of sync. My schoolmates had moved on, and I was left behind. No one seemed to realize that if I was going to reintegrate into the rhythm of my education, I needed much help and guidance. Yet I received none.

I couldn't get into the routine of the schoolwork; my mind, once so sharp and excited to learn new things, now felt strangely noisy, yet dull. Some people in school stared at me and whispered; I knew they had heard about my suicide attempt.

I became distracted and gave up; the usual friends would go off campus to drink and smoke at lunch. I wasn't healed from the suicide attempt, and no one had helped me to escape the demons that were haunting my everyday existence. I wasn't healed from the trauma of my first boyfriend; I tried to forget the date rape had ever happened and never labeled it that way. I shoved the memory down under the surface with great effort and moved on.

I started going out with a young guy my age. He was also into partying, and we would go out on weekends with his friends.

Eventually, the partying spread into weekdays for him and his friends, and their lives became one long party.

I still had my conscience pulling on me hard to attend school. I chose to go to school during the week but partied on weekends. Amazingly, I still felt the inner nudge, "Don't throw away your future; get back into it."

I fought hard to get back to normal, study, and stay in school. However, I was troubled, traumatized, demonized, and needed help. I didn't know it then, but I needed God.

I was drowning in dark waters, desperately grabbing at anything that might prevent me from going under one more time, anything that may help me stop choking on the water I swallowed as I gasped for breath. I understood why they say, "A heart can break." My heart was broken, and I felt the pain physically.

I also felt a suffocating disappointment; it felt like my lungs were constricted, and I was never able to inhale deeply.

I never wanted to be about "that" life.

I thought I was smarter than that, but I wasn't. Here I was, skipping school and hanging out with people with no future. Something else was running my life, especially if I consumed alcohol.

They say that youth is wasted on the young. Many of the most terrible decisions are made in our youth; some can not be undone and follow us for the rest of our lives. I was working overtime at bad decisions.

Daytime drinking parties during school at my friends' homes were a weekly event, and I was easily convinced to ditch to attend them. While parents were at work, they had no clue that their homes were filled with teenagers dancing, drinking, smoking, and hanging out.

There was a girl that I didn't know at one of these parties. She was particularly friendly with me, bringing me a beer and asking if I needed anything, so I was friendly with her. I thought it was a bit strange, but I shrugged it off.

I left the party, and later that day, she made the mistake of very matter-of-factly telling one of my friends at the party, "I was with her boyfriend last night."

Of course, my friend couldn't wait to tell me. She immediately found me at my home, filled me in, and announced, "You have to get her; you can't let her disrespect you like that!"

"She's right", I thought. The school was a dog-eat-dog world; I had to defend my pride. She made me look like a fool, and I was angry. I had to do something about it.

The following day at school, early in the morning, freshly showered, leaning back on the hood of my car, I nervously hit my bent knee with my rolled-up homework.

I had parked in front of the school, waiting for her to arrive. Looking around, I noticed more people than usual in front of the school, not going onto campus, just hanging around. They also seemed to be waiting for something to happen; some looked my way and whispered. I realized everyone knew what she had done and were waiting around to see what I would do about being disrespected.

My friend who was egging me on was right there next to me, nervously puffing on a cigarette. She was the first to notice that this girl had been dropped off and was walking down the sidewalk towards the school entrance. "There she is, there she is!" My friend said excitedly. I suddenly realized this girl was taller and bigger than me; she hadn't looked so big the day before.

    I knew I had to confront her or lose my reputation and look like a punk. I called her name, and she turned around and smiled as I approached her, "Were you with my boyfriend?" I asked directly.

    She stood up to me and said, "Yeah, I was," moving close to me.

    "Then why did you act all friendly with me yesterday? You made me look like a fool." I cussed her out, and my martial arts were second nature. In a couple of quick moves, I punched her, ripped her blouse off, and knocked her to the ground. She wet her pants. She sat on the ground, humiliated. I kept telling her, "Get up!" but she refused.

    The crowd that ran to watch the "fight" was cheering and congratulating me. I was cursing at her, telling her to get up, and acting tough, but I felt wrong inside. I looked at her sitting on the ground, and my eyes met hers. I wasn't proud of myself; this fight was different. Since I had no alcohol in my body, I wasn't filled with rage. I was thinking rationally and had soberly done what I thought I had to do to survive at this school. I felt sorry for this girl.

    I walked to class, but the attendance officers came later that day and took me into the vice principal's office. I swallowed hard and entered the office, which felt dim and shadowy. The large picture window, with partially closed Venetian blinds, cast eerie shadows on the heavy furniture, creating an ominous atmosphere.

The girl sat beside her mother, who sat quietly with her shoulders hunched over. The oversized wingback chair seemed to swallow her small frame. She glanced up at me blankly as I walked in, then back at the vice principal. She looked beat and weary. I was ashamed and wished I could apologize to this humble elderly woman. I knew what it felt like to be in her shoes, humiliated in a principal's office.

From behind his imposing desk, the vice principal was blunt and straightaway asked me, "Why did you beat her down?"

I hadn't taken my seat yet; looking directly at him, I told him what she had done and how she was bragging to everyone, making me look stupid.

Surprisingly, he took my side and told her, "You don't disrespect people in the neighborhood; you give them no choice; they have to defend their pride." I was not in the neighborhood, but some of my friends were, and so was my boyfriend.

Truth be told, I felt so bad about what I had done that I wanted him to reprimand me, but he didn't. Ultimately, we were both suspended, but no one was available to pick me up from school, so the vice principal took me in his bright yellow sports car to my home on the other side of the tracks.

As we got to my apartments, he realized I did not come from a financially well-off home. I could tell by his comments that he supposed that my family was dysfunctional, maybe on drugs. Families living in these kinds of apartments are broken; they frequent prison, are violent, are alcoholics, and most likely are one-parent homes. However, my family was hard-working and decent. Mother and Father were present, and we had to show respect and manners in our home. We were required and expected to act responsibly and do chores. My friends loved my home atmosphere because of this. They said I had good parents.

Many years later, my family would fall into dysfunction, but at this point, I was the only troublemaker in my home.

I knew he sensed I was not okay; I felt his pity as he half-heartedly encouraged me to try harder at school. He then dropped me off on my long driveway. I stood alone, watching his sports car speed off; I inhaled deeply and walked in defeat to my apartment. Another day, another mess I had created.

I was crying out for help, but no one was listening.

I later learned that the girl I had beaten up had to go to another school; she could not face the humiliation. I had become the "mean girl" and was not proud of myself.

"Remember your Creator while you are young [in the days of your youth], before the days of trouble [evil] come and the years when you say, "I find no pleasure [delight] in them." Ecclesiastes 12:1 EXB

Chapter 22

Did You Hear That The Overdose Left Her Crazy?

Being "canceled" is something that has always been done in society. Surrender to the powers that be, give in to peer pressure, follow the group's rules, or you will be ostracized, blackballed, and marked. I had to defend myself; all it took was one person making a fool out of you, and you'd lose respect. I had witnessed friends distance themselves from the person that had been canceled, not wanting to be identified with them, not wanting to be associated with the person who lost face, lest they also be out of the group of friends, untouchable, and blacklisted overnight. I did not want to be canceled.

I was still having a tough time adjusting to school. On this day, the campus was quiet and peaceful; the students were in class. I could not bear to be in class, so I sat on a cement bench right in the middle of campus, enjoying the warm breeze on my face, waiting for my friend to get out of gym class so we could go get lunch off campus. I needed to breathe, and I was getting restless and felt the air in the class was lacking in oxygen.

The gym was located about 60 yards across from me, but I could see the door from where I chose to sit. She poked her head out the gym side door and signaled with her hands that she would be out in a bit. So I mouthed, "Okay, I'll wait right here."

Well, apparently, another girl had seen me, and she spread the word in the school that the suicide attempt had made me crazy and that now I just sit alone at school "talking to myself."

The gym doors swung open and my friend walked towards me. We both headed to the parking lot for lunch. I hadn't even buckled my seatbelt yet. She immediately asked me, "Do you know what is being said about you?" while handing me a beer from the back seat.

"No, I don't know," I replied, opening the beer. I didn't want it; why was I taking it? Why was I opening it? Why was I unable to say no?

"What now?" I thought and refocused back on what my friend was saying. We arrived at the burger joint, and she began to fill me in on who said what to whom as I ordered my food. I rolled my eyes, getting more and more aggravated by the minute. She enthusiastically relayed every juicy detail concerning what "EVERYBODY" was saying about me.

I was angered and threw my just-purchased food in the trash without even taking a bite. We had come in her car. I got in and slammed the door, and she followed me quickly; I don't think she expected this response.

"Take me back to the school to confront the girl spreading this gossip."

My friend became very nervous and pleaded, "Leave it alone. She will be with all her homegirls, and it's just me and you." Her voice was shaking. I would have been scared, too, if I had any sense, but rage had taken over.

The girl who said this about me hung out in front of the school on a particular wall with her homegirls (The girls whom everyone feared and tiptoed around to avoid conflict with.) I had seen them beat a girl down in the cafeteria, leaving her all scratched up in the face, permanently scarred. Another time, they had jumped a girl in the bathroom, leaving her bruised and bleeding, crying on the floor.

I didn't care, even if they all jumped me. I would focus on the one girl who was telling people that I had gone crazy. "I'll show her crazy!" I said.

"Stop the car in front of the school," I told my friend.

She was there with her homegirls, standing against the same wall. I got out of the car and didn't wait for my friend to get off (to her relief, I believe). I walked directly up to the girl and began challenging her with what she said about me.

I was furious but fully expecting to have them all jump me. I had seen it before, but instead, a couple of the older girls began to mediate. Saying, "Naw man, she has respect for you. She wouldn't say that." and thankfully, they started talking me down from my anger. The girl apologized, and the other girls said, "It's cool, you're cool with us.". This all puzzled me, but later, when I could think clearly, I was grateful, "What was I thinking?" Like always, when I became angry, I blacked out, and the truth is, I was not thinking.

The adults around me observed me closely at school and home; I felt their eyes. I needed someone to talk to me, to bring up the suicide attempt. I needed to know someone cared about me. I needed someone to trust, someone I could open up to. I was still a ticking time bomb. I got secretive, puzzled looks. I felt their pity, curiosity, and maybe even judgmental disapproval. However, no one opened up a meaningful conversation with me. I just felt their eyes on my every move.

Suicides happen in clusters. I learned that three other girls had attempted suicide after I had. Two guys had also attempted suicide. The girls, like myself, had failed. Tragically, however, the guys had succeeded in their attempt. One young man who was very popular at school had driven off a cliff under the influence of alcohol and marijuana. The other young man went missing for a while. He was known for being dark in his mood, listening to heavy metal, wearing metal shirts, and also spending his days high on weed. His friends and family asked around for his whereabouts, but no one knew where he was. Sadly, he was later found under a bridge with a shotgun in his mouth.

I learned about this after I began socializing again, mainly with my baddie friends who always had partying on their minds.

This is called a suicide cluster, caused by social learning from nearby individuals. I felt guilty. Did I trigger this suicide cluster? This deeply impacted me, and I felt responsible for the harm that came to these individuals. This guilt added to my misery.

However, this doesn't take into account the spiritual aspect of life. I know from experience that we live amongst spiritual beings; there are spirits that are entirely evil and take joy in destroying, deforming, and twisting our lives. If possible, they will start when we are small. I became acutely aware of the presence of this spiritual evil in my life and the lives of those around me—deforming personalities of once happy, joyful youth - turning them into bitter, hard, broken, self-destructive, rebellious youth. There was always a reason. Everyone had a story that no one bothered to hear. However, at this point, I wasn't aware of anything that could counter this evil that surrounded me. I wondered if there was an answer. If there was hope or if this was it. Life stunk as far as I could see, and there was no hope of it getting better.

No one is an island unto themselves.

We do affect each other; we influence one another. I understand now that I can become someone's hope, someone's light. I see the importance of surrounding yourself with positive, godly people. But at the time, I felt like I was on a fast-moving, runaway train, and I was not the conductor. I had no idea who was, but I did sense it was evil and had my total and complete destruction in mind. I lived with a heavy foreboding.

I tried hard to "do right." I woke daily with a resolve to go to class, not ditch, and to stay away from alcohol. I tried to become the same optimistic, "No one is going to break me" young lady I used to be. However, if you could see into the spirit, you would see heavy chains that had me imprisoned, evil demons that were now in control of certain areas of my life. Other folks call them "diseases," "habits," "mental illnesses," and "issues". However, I had seen these entities looking back at me from my own eyes; I felt them; I sensed the evil. I was helpless against them.

There were a few decent young men who were interested in me. The one my parents wanted me to marry comes to mind. He was a fireman and was looking to settle down. He had pursued me very respectfully for about one year. I saw the good in him and how much he respected and valued me.

He was handsome but not arrogant. My parents liked that he was educated, very decent, and had a good head on his shoulders. He spoke to my parents and told them he wanted to marry me one day. He had a 3-year plan. He had become a firefighter; then, he was in the process of purchasing a house. Then he wanted to marry me. I had managed to act "normal" around him for about one year. He lived far away, and when he came to see me, it was always with a lot of respect. We would all go to a museum or the beach. We'd visit beautiful parks or the theatre. Other times, we hung out at my home, always with the family present.

But the time came when I was so dark that I couldn't hide what my life had become anymore. I felt as though my life was no longer my own. He came to visit me at my home. I walked in with my boyfriend; we were obviously up to no good. His eyes were bloodshot from drinking and smoking weed.

"Look who is here to visit you," Mom said.

I just said, "Hey," and ignored him. Then, my boyfriend and I walked out of the house, leaving my family there to explain my rude actions.

I didn't think I deserved anything good, wholesome, or decent. I felt that I was ruined and felt like garbage.

Remember the edge of the pit that I once tried so hard not to fall into? Well, I can't tell you exactly when it happened, but I fell in deep. I now found myself groping my way in the darkness!

I started drinking daily and became even more interested in the new age. I now had to read my horoscope all the time. I was drawn to dark things. When I drank, I felt evil entities around me. Sometimes, when I looked in the mirror, I saw them looking out at me from my own eyes. It no longer alarmed me. It became my "normal". I also began to black out when I drank.

At this point, I was really lost and in deep depression. When I drank, I started fights wherever I went. I had become that one friend you didn't want to bring along because she always ruined everything.

On one occasion, a "Peace Concert" was held at the park, promoting non-violence in our city. I don't remember exactly what happened, but I was told later that a young lady from out of town looked at me wrong. I broke a bottle and went after her with it; I ruined the concert and caused a big scene.

So unlike me, or was this who I was now? Maybe I was a loser that wasn't supposed to amount to anything. I wasn't sure anymore. All I knew was that I was no longer in control. I had a facade that all was well. However, deep inside, I was just an empty shell. My soul was tattered and dying.

The next day after the concert fiasco, I walked into art class, and the guys started humming the theme song from "Rocky." My face flushed as I hurriedly found my seat. The scary part of this incident was that I had no memory of what I had done the night before.

I became very hostile, and there was now a compulsion to drink alcohol daily.

Compulsion. That word would describe what was driving me now. I felt as though I had lost control of my life, surroundings, school, and now even my person.

I had a strong pull towards pornography, but fortunately, it was not readily available. I didn't have access to it. I could see how this may have become another compulsion, though.

My only memory of exposure to porn was a few times as a preteen. I ran into a page in an open field where the neighborhood children used to have "rock wars."

"I don't understand why anyone would take these sorts of photos," I thought in my naive twelve-year-old mind. At the same time, I was scared by the hypnotic power these images had to draw me in. Just the fact that I was drawn so strongly caused me to believe I was an immoral, dirty person. I felt defective.

Something real had attached itself to me. I felt its strong pull after the date rape at fifteen. I also felt a compulsion towards promiscuity, especially if I consumed alcohol.

Still, I fought hard not to become "that girl" who would jump from guy to guy. I did pretty well in that department, but because I felt no worth, I knew I teetered between fighting and giving up. I could have easily not cared anymore. I could easily give in to the compulsions if I stopped fighting.

Something kept me fighting. Maybe it was the morals my Grandma Maria and Mom had instilled in me as a child. I'm not sure, but I tried hard to remain abstinent.

I knew my life was ruined; I had messed it up beyond repair. Feelings that no one cared about me were overwhelming. It dawned on me that the spiritual evil that had almost killed me through suicide was still present. I called it "Aunt Maggie". It hadn't given up on destroying me. Evil entities were fighting for complete control of my being. Every week, I became worse and worse; they had me in their grip, and I didn't like who I had become.

By this point, I went out with my friends almost daily, which always involved alcohol. After drinking and hanging out with friends, I often went home and passed out on my bed. My mom came home from work to find me fully clothed and unconscious. She'd go into a desperate panic, trying to wake me up.

"Maria, what did you take?" Shaking me, she'd say, "Are you overdosing?" She'd then call my friends and question them, "What did Maria take?" "Please tell me, she won't be in trouble; I just want to ensure this isn't another suicide attempt." Her frantic voice revealed panic and desperation. My poor mom worried that I might be overdosing again, that I had tried to commit suicide again.

The enemy of my soul had his talons deep into me. He hadn't taken my life that day, long before when he moved me to overdose.

But just as the demon threatened when I came out of the coma, "You think you got away, you traitor? I'm going to get you!"

This evil enemy didn't give up. It continued to control me and twist me, pervert me, enslave me. Maybe it didn't kill me quickly that day that I overdosed. But it didn't leave; no one made it go. So, it settled for killing me slowly.

Darkness took over my life. I began to do peculiar things and found ways to drink without being obvious. I'd hide a bottle of hard liquor outside my bedroom window by tying it with a rope to pull it back when I wanted a drink.

I had to have my room ice cold. My sister says I would bark out orders to them. "Get me some water!" and if they didn't jump to do it, I would grab their arms and dig my nails into them. A stream of curse words would come pouring out of my mouth. I looked at them with hateful eyes and hurled insults using filthy language. I was mean, cruel, and violent.

Chapter 23
The Depth of My Bondage

Many years later, while spending some time with my sisters, I expressed annoyance at someone using very foul language in front of us.

One of my sisters reminded me, "Remember when you used to talk to us that way?"

"What? No, I didn't remember.

 She went on to tell me in detail how I abused and intimidated them. I didn't remember this; I wept in deep sorrow. I have no memory of ever doing these things! How bound was I? What else had I done that I didn't remember?

I became an alcoholic. My first thought in the morning was to get a drink.

Almost daily, my friends came by, honking their horns, and without a word, I was out the door on my way to party. I was drinking my life away. This was another familiar spirit from my family. Many family members had lost all to alcohol. Despite being educated and reaching prestige and financial prosperity, they had lost it all behind alcohol, including their family and eventually their lives. This was my future if nothing changed. I needed help.

I had lost my moral compass; I became very self-destructive. After having the first drink of alcohol, I'd wait for that familiar warmth. Then, looking in the mirror, I'd see those eyes, evil, smug, and mocking.

Just recently, on a trip with my family to "The Happiest Place on Earth" - Disneyland, I asked my daughter as we walked up Main Street, "Do you want to know something about me that you didn't know?"

"What?" She said, looking at me curiously.

"I've been arrested in Disneyland and taken to Disney jail."

Giggling nervously, she said, "For what?"

"For being a drunken fool, being obnoxious, and standing up on the rides," I said.

My adult kids and grandkids cannot believe I lived that life. They say it's not like me at all. It was not like me then, either. I was gone; I had become someone else. Someone who had lost her way.

I was diving head-first into quick destruction. However, something happened that caused me to put on the brakes.

There was a new drug in town; it was different, and many friends were getting hooked. It was a scary drug; it caused some friends to go crazy, and some were institutionalized in a mental hospital. I feared actually losing my mind and determined to stay away from it.

My boyfriend seemed very traumatized himself. He was my age. We were two very lost teens. He came from a decent family, but I could feel his pain. He was an excellent baseball player and football player, and he had been scouted to play pro ball. He was a good student and had gone to a military academy. However, he seemed to be running hard to outrun something painful in his own soul.

 I went to prom with him and all his friends and their girlfriends. We were all dressed in beautiful, expensive ball gowns. We met at someone's house and took many photos, but the actual prom disappointed me. We danced and took the "prom picture," but it did not live up to the hype. My boyfriend and his friends stepped out and smoked some "angel dust" and returned totally toasted. It turned into a nightmare of an evening.

 Afterward, we all went to his house for an after-party. The smoke-filled room reeked of "Sherms" (Marijuana dipped in embalming fluid). Everyone was high; I wasn't and wanted to go home, but my boyfriend refused to take me home.

 He became threatening, so I sat quietly on the sofa. As they continued smoking and drinking, I watched the darkened room fill up with morphing characters. As the night wore on, his friends were moving awkwardly, in their individual intoxicated realities, dressed in messy formal attire.

 Once again, I sensed demons - evil puppet masters in the room. The people weren't even communicating anymore. It wasn't that they weren't speaking to one another, but that they were all on different trips.

 Watching all these people under the influence "tripping" was a mind-bending experience. I sat in place holding a beer the whole night. Music played in the background, and eventually, conversations ceased.

I was paranoid, and strangely, I felt that the demons in the room hadn't noticed me yet. I didn't dare make a noise; I didn't want to be seen.

He and his friends got plastered. These new drugs were game changers. Supercools, shermans, angel dust: I couldn't get into them. I watched my happy, quick-witted friends get hooked and go completely catatonic sometimes. They became anti-social loners who would go out into the field by themselves, smoke these drugs, and stay out there all day tripping. They lost their personality and connection to all friendships and relationships, and some eventually lost their mind.

As I mentioned before, I have always been sensitive to the spiritual, even when I didn't have Christ in my life. Whenever I was sober around people who were high on drugs or alcohol, I was able to sense the spirit acting out through them. I understand why bars advertise the sale of alcohol as "spirits." That's precisely what is being sold—a spiritual experience. You loan yourself to a demon for the night. That's why you find yourself doing things you would never do sober.

That particular evening after prom was memorable in a sad way. I kept my drinking in moderation; I refused to get high; I guess you can say I got scared straight. I also didn't want anything to do with sex. I wanted to leave. I considered walking home, but walking in the dark, in a full ball gown, about five miles, was out of the question.

After acting disgusted with me because I was not partying with them, my boyfriend threatened me a couple of times if I tried to leave. He was a nice, caring guy, but drugs were changing him. Normally, I wouldn't feel threatened, but alcohol changed everything. He seemed to become someone else, and his eyes became foreign.

Throughout the night, he continued to party hard and ignored me. I kept asking him to take me home, but he wouldn't.

When he finally took me home, he had sobered up some; it was six in the morning. He was a bit apologetic and tried to walk me to my door. I wasn't waiting for him; I exited the car and rushed to my apartment gate. Just then, my father walked out of the house on his way to work. I was so relieved to be home. I was a bit scared and wanted to tell my Dad what had happened. As I tried to go through our gate into our yard, my Dad shoved me against the fence and angrily told me, "If you can stay out late doing God knows what with your boyfriend and think that he can just bring you home like nothing he can just take you and support you because I won't be your fool."

Dad looked at me with disgust and told me to leave, "You can't live here anymore!" I couldn't believe my Dad had knocked me into the fence. His shove would have knocked me to the ground if the fence wasn't there. I was hurt; he had always been gentle with me. I wanted him to tell me, "I'm glad you are home safe," and ask, "Are you okay?" "I wanted him to protect me."

But instead, he got in his car and angrily drove away.

Holding in my tears, I rushed into the house and started packing a few things into a bag. My mom was behind me, saying,

"Don't go." I pulled stuff out of my closet; my little sisters and younger brother watched in confusion. "Your Dad was just angry; he didn't mean it; just let him get over it."

My Dad had never treated me this way; we had always had a good relationship. He didn't communicate much with me or anyone in the house, but I always knew he loved me. That day, our relationship changed. It felt as though he wrote me off; this wounded me deeply. This experience with my Dad scarred me.

After this point, my boyfriend wasn't attending school anymore. When he was sober, he was a nice guy; we could talk and discuss life, and he was very understanding and kind. However, he was now trapped in addiction and spent the days with his friends shooting heroin and the evenings partying at someone's house. I was not aware of the heroin, and I didn't know how bad things had gotten in his life.

We didn't ask his parents if I could stay at their house. I packed a few things and got in his car. We drove in silence as we headed for his house. I waited in the car as he went in and told his parents I had nowhere to live, so I'd be staying there.

His parents both worked, so it was just he and I in the house. We both chose to skip school, and now that I was around him all the time, I realized that he partied daily. I began to get scared. I thought, "One day, we will have no way back to normal life."

Then I thought, "Maybe we already had gone too far, and now all doors had been closed to us." I began to believe we had no choice in the mess we had made of our young lives. I felt trapped.

I already knew he was drinking alcohol and smoking weed, but he then got into heavier drugs. We were both angry and miserable. Alcohol had become normal to both of us long ago. For some reason, though, being in this atmosphere of heavy drug use and the loss I felt without my own family caused me to resist getting high.

No matter how crazy things got outside, I always had "normal" to come home to. Now, we had no one stopping us. We were on the edge, and I feared falling off. I even managed to resist alcohol in this season. However, that monster would come back with a vengeance later on.

I had made bad choices after bad choices, so I was responsible for what my life had come to. Yet somehow, I could not seem to be able to make good choices. I felt traumatized, and every poor choice brought more trauma, and I became more and more unable to be proactive in correcting my disastrous life.

I was living at my boyfriend's house, sleeping in their living room; I didn't want to be there. Although his family was kind to me, they were never actually asked if I could move in, yet here I was.

My boyfriend didn't mind me being there, but he had the upper hand because of how it happened. It left me needing a place to stay; I had no voice to set boundaries or a choice to tell him anything.

When his parents were at work, he and his friends got plastered regularly on alcohol and "angel dust." This was his home, and I had moved in uninvited. I was miserable. I wanted to leave so badly.

I felt that knot in the pit of my stomach constantly and stayed awake at night weeping and wishing I could go home. I started talking to God, "God, I want to start my life over."

"What happened to me? How did I end up here?" I wished so badly that I could have a fresh start.

God was setting up some circumstances to soften my heart. He was making a path that led directly to him. However, I could not see this then. I only saw hopelessness, misery, and a dead-end street going nowhere. I had no reason to wake up in the morning, but somehow I did, always hoping that today would be the day I would find peace.

Somehow, my being homeless had been another wake-up call of sorts. It opened my eyes to where my life was headed, the cold reality of it all. Pretty much everyone around us had begun to use drugs regularly, following in the footsteps of the older homeboys and some of the older homegirls.

I refused to take hard drugs; I reasoned that I was barely making it as it was. How much deeper would I fall if I got into heavy drugs? It took all I had to hang on to life. I feared this strange new lifestyle. I felt broken but determined I would not remain broken.

There was something extremely evil with these new drugs. They were next-level. I sometimes saw these demons whenever friends lit up and smoked. I wondered if anyone else could see them but didn't dare ask.

I missed the stability of my home.

My boyfriend used them, and they changed him. It was scary to witness. While under the influence, which was more and more often, my boyfriend began to mistreat me.

Chapter 24

Threatened With A Knife

On one extremely challenging day, I found myself pacing the room, feeling like my heart would explode from sheer disappointment. I could take no more. He walked in, and I told him sadly, "I want to leave." Turning to look at me with a strange, blank stare, he said nothing. His eyes were red and glassy. I knew he had been drinking and smoking marijuana. Without a word, he quietly turned and walked out of the room. I heard him in the kitchen.

"Maybe he gets it; maybe he understands that this is not right and that we aren't good for each other," I thought.

The bedroom door swung open abruptly. He threw me on the bed and jumped on top of me, holding a large kitchen knife to my throat.

He told me, "You want to leave? You want to leave, huh?" clenching his teeth. " If you leave, I will kill you! If I can't have you, nobody can." He wasn't shouting, but I could feel each word being pushed out forcefully.

I looked into his scary eyes, filled with rage. His eyebrows were in a deep scowl; his face was right by mine, almost forehead to forehead. His face beaded with sweat. He smelled of alcohol and weed. His breathing was rapid and deep as he held the knife to my throat, pressing the sharp edge against my skin.

Who was this? I didn't recognize him. Shocked and terrified by the suddenness of the experience, I was freaking out inside but managed to keep calm. "I was only saying that because I want you to stop using angel dust. I'm not going anywhere." I added calmly, "Plus, where am I going to go? I have nowhere to go." He just held the knife to my throat without speaking. I'm sure it was just minutes, but it seemed like an eternity.

My calm response calmed him, and he took the knife off my throat. He got off me and walked out of the room.

He had never really been violent with me, so this was shocking. He wasn't in a rage. He seemed calm when he left the room to get the knife. This incident made me determined to get out of there; next time, I may not be able to talk my way out of it.

He never acknowledged what he had done, "Does he even realize what he did?" I wondered. He walked around the house silently, keeping a close eye on me. He always kept me in his peripheral vision. He continued to drink and smoke weed daily.

One day, I waited until he was busy doing something else out in the garage and secretly got on the house phone. Keeping an eye towards the back door, I dialed up a friend who lived in a different city. The phone rang: one, two, three, four… pick up! Pick up! I mouthed silently, angry at how loud the phone seemed. She finally picked up, and I quickly told her what was going on in my life, afraid he would catch me on the phone.

"That's terrible; you don't have to put up with that," she said "Come stay with me; my parents won't care."

I exhaled as I hung up the phone, relieved that I had made the call successfully and had somewhere to go. I waited until he was distracted, got a few of my belongings, and quickly shoved them in my purse.

I found a moment of privacy and opened up to his cousin, "He's becoming violent when he drinks; I'm frightened and want to leave." I told her about my friend who invited me to live with her. She seemed to understand and suggested, "Tell him you are coming to work with me, then have your friend pick you up there." That's precisely what I did. I was grateful to her for helping me get out of a very toxic and dangerous situation.

I was relieved to be out of there, but now I was again going to be living in someone else's home.

Living in a big, beautiful home

It was a brand new build, a beautiful, six-bedroom, five-bathroom home. This was a foreign world to me. Her family had everything they needed and then some.

Her mom called me to the kitchen and asked me to sit on one of the stools. As we talked, she made me an offer to stay with them permanently, "We'll put you through college and support you. All we ask is that you stay away from your boyfriend." I agreed, and it was great for a few months.

My friend's brothers were the sweetest; they waited on her hand and foot and did the same for me now. They'd ask if I wanted anything from restaurants or the store.

But soon, my friend became jealous that she was not the only girl in the family anymore. She began to mistreat me. She became very rude and cruel to me. I only had a few belongings. She had a huge, beautiful room with a large closet filled with clothes and shoes. The vanity drawers in her bathroom were filled with makeup and every kind of product you could think of. Yet she would get my makeup and tell me, "You can't tell me anything; I'm letting you stay in my house!" She was correct; I couldn't tell her anything; I was at her mercy. "I don't want you on my bed. You can sleep on the floor." She announced one evening, looking at me with a disgusted look on her face.

Then, there were days when she asked sarcastically, "When are you going to leave? I didn't want you here; I just felt sorry for you."

It was demeaning to be treated this way, and I had flashbacks to when I was four, and my aunt pretended not to know us and didn't want us in her home.

However, her family was good to me and included me in the family. Although I never took it, her Mom even offered me spending money when she knew that I was going out. Her brothers offered to wash my laundry; the family always waited for me at the dinner table before they began a meal. However, the more her family accepted me, the worse my friend treated me.

Her home was beautiful, spacious, and finely furnished. They shopped every week and came home with bags and bags from high-end shops; many times, the bags remained in the closet without being touched, and many of my friend's clothing hung in the closet with the price tag still on them.

Sadly, after dinner, like clockwork, her mom would sit on the sofa in the spacious living room and pour herself a glass of expensive liquor every evening. Keeping the bottle by her side to refill her glass, she'd begin to call her husband, "Come here!" He would come to her from wherever he was. "Sit down!" She'd order, her speech slurring. He would sit on the couch across from her. She then loudly and cruelly berated him for hours. He'd just look at her.

Everyone stayed in their bedroom and pretended it wasn't happening.

It was a routine, almost a nightly occurrence. I never heard her husband respond; It was very strange to me. I thought of my quiet, kind, respectful mom and my quiet dad. I had never seen either of them drunk nor heard them cuss; if they disagreed, they did it privately, and we were seldom aware of it.

In that beautiful, lavish home, I learned that money can buy many material things, but money is not the answer for a turbulent soul searching for peace.

My friend's cruelty intensified, and once again, I was not in a position to do anything about it. I was in her home.

I felt trapped and out of my element again. I secretly cried and wondered what was wrong with me. My father had thrown me out of my home. Was I really this worthless?

We went to parties with her friends and her crowd; I knew no one in this community. I just went along, played the part, and acted like I was having "so much fun!"

Driving to these beautiful homes was always an experience that impressed me. My eyes darted back and forth, taking in all the details of these extravagant, immaculate homes.

Of course, I assumed erroneously that more affluence equaled more life satisfaction. However, as I looked closer, the void soon came into view, the endless search for purpose that led to a constant need for consumption. The resulting misery and disappointment in their lives were apparent. I was familiar with the chasing after meaning, satisfaction, the pursuit of happiness, and the desperation in not finding it. I recognized it in them, different neighborhoods, the same chasing after the wind…

One evening at one of these parties, sitting around the kitchen, drinking wine, talking, and laughing, I looked around the room, feeling strangely detached. I just watched everyone around me and felt no connection to these people and no joy in the festivities. Mouths moved, but the conversation was not registering. I stopped following their conversation, and suddenly, a rush of emotion and sadness hit me.

Wearied of the now permanent lump in my throat, I could not bear to sit there pretending any longer. I got up, slipped out of the party, and walked down the driveway. The front yard was expansive. The house was located deep in the lot. I found a quiet spot and sat on the wooden fence far from the others. I couldn't even hear the party in the house.

Tears began to pour out of my eyes, turning into a constant flow that I didn't even try to stop. I felt a dam break. The sprinklers turned on for a bit, bringing that familiar, beautiful scent of wet earth and wet vegetation. The smell of the flowers increased. The familiar scents brought my family to my mind. My, was I homesick! I couldn't help but notice the irony: such a beautiful home in a gorgeous neighborhood. It was a "good" party with nice people, yet none of that could penetrate my soul nor fill the profound emptiness in me.

    Gazing at innumerable stars, I wondered, "Is God up there?" feeling small and insignificant. I turned my gaze down the dark, tree-lined street. It was almost empty; I inhaled deeply, feeling extreme sadness. Feeling broken and lost. I realized I was trapped, but then this is what my life had become: one big trap.

    After this party, I would be going back to my friend's house. She seemed to take increasing pleasure in humiliating me. The thought came, "She treats me like her mom treats her dad." I had become her emotional punching bag.

    I was deep in thought; again, my heart still literally, physically hurt from so much sadness. I missed my family. I missed our shabby little apartment and sitting with them after dinner on our ugly orange, rust, and brown plaid sofa watching "Wheel of Fortune" or some other silly program.

    I suddenly became aware of someone standing beside me. "You okay?" she asked. I shook my head but couldn't get any words out. "What's wrong?" It was one of her friends, a beautiful girl with green eyes, who also seemed to have everything going for her. She'd noticed I had walked outside. Curious, she followed and found me sitting alone.

    I was guarded and seldom trusted anyone with my personal story, but her question was sincere. I found myself confiding my situation with her. "I'm trying to figure out what to do; my friend turned on me. She humiliates me daily. I know she doesn't want me there anymore."

"Why don't you come to stay with me?" She asked matter-of-factly, catching me off guard. I looked at her, and to my surprise, I quickly responded, "Yes." Even to this day, I don't know what either of us was thinking, but I know I was desperate and appreciated her kindness. I had no plan; I was in survival mode and did the next available thing.

I found myself in a strange city where I didn't belong and had no way home.

I let my friend know that I would not be going back to her home. I was glad to have an "out" from an unbearable situation. We got in my new friend's white sedan, and off I went to her home, crazy as it sounds! I was not raised this way, and neither did my relatives live like this. I was the black sheep of the family, and understandably my "antics" were always the topic of conversation.

It was late; we opened the front door and walked into her unfamiliar home in the dark. I followed behind her too closely, bumping into her. We both laughed as we felt our way inside and into a bedroom with bunk beds. Still not turning on any lights, she said, "You sleep in that one; I'll sleep over here." Barely able to see her hand, I strained to see where she was pointing. We both lay down fully clothed, and I quickly drifted off to sleep.

The next thing I knew, I was awakened in the morning by a young guy staring at my eyelashes stuck on the nightstand beside where I lay. He then immediately ran out and yelled, "Mom! There's some girl in my room!" I sat straight up; my friend was gone, and I could hear muffled voices coming from somewhere in the house. I recognized one of them as hers but didn't remember her name. "I think it was a flower, Daisy? Or was it Pearl? What was her name?" I had to use the restroom but had no idea where I was.

There were two doors in the room, but I did not dare open either of them; what if one was to a bedroom or something? So I just sat and waited for my friend "what's her name" to come and get me.

She eventually did. She showed me to the restroom, took me to the kitchen, and introduced me to her Mom, who was busy cooking. She was also kind, and I saw where my friend got her beauty. She resembled her mom with the same light green eyes.

The next day, my new friend would drive me over to where I had been staying to pick up the few pieces of clothing that belonged to me and to thank the family for their kindness in allowing me to live there and their offer to put me through college.

A particular impression that stands out to me is how empty and sad my new, beautiful friend seemed. She seemed to have everything, yet I couldn't recall a sadder heart, not even those with nothing going for them. What was this deep sadness I perceived? I would stare at her, trying to figure out what it was, but it remained a mystery.

Her entire family treated me well. I settled in as much as possible and stayed there through the summer. We would go out and party every weekend, sometimes even on weekdays.

She took me to some apartments, where I met her "other group" of friends. They partied hard, and I recall feeling that she did not belong there. We were exposed to some sketchy situations.

I met this pretty, slim British girl with long blond hair. She was very pregnant but still drank with us and got high on whatever was available to smoke. She grabbed at it aggressively before it was even passed to her. I felt like she despised herself.

On one occasion, we were partying in the apartment, and someone called us to the kitchen, "Quick, come get her!"

We walked in as she banged her baby bump hard against the corner of the kitchen counter, saying, "I don't want this baby." She seemed set on destroying herself.

I later learned that her stepdad had violated her, resulting in this pregnancy.

No one knows the pain carried by those who surround us.

She hadn't told her Mom, but it was eating her up. After her baby was born, she continued to self-destruct. She lived in a drug-induced haze.

My friend and I continued to go party at these chaotic apartments. These parties always ended in conflict and violence.

On one occasion, there was a disagreement with a neighbor. After it seemingly calmed down, an individual returned and started shooting into the house through the windows! The curtains blew in spurts, and with every flying bullet, glass flew everywhere, and people scrambled, shouting and running to get their guns to retaliate.

From the hallway, amid the chaos, my eye caught a glimpse of the British girl's baby. She was lying on the bed by herself, screaming at the top of her lungs. Terrified, her little body flinched and recoiled with every gunshot as glass hit her face red from crying. In the confusion and noise, I grabbed the baby and hid in the closet, the bullets still shattering glass and ripping through curtains.

I sat in the dark closet for what seemed like an eternity, holding the baby and covering her ears while my heart pounded in mine.

I hadn't heard sirens but spied some blue and red lights flashing from under the closet door. I heard an authoritative voice shouting orders. I came out of the closet, relieved that the police had arrived. I looked around, the curtains were now completely off the wall. The shattered window was exposed, and I could see outside where patrol cars were parked, and police officers were making some arrests. They then started up towards the apartment. I quickly gave the baby to her mother, and my friend and I were able to leave in the confusion.

Whoa, what in the world! This was intense, and I did not want this to become my "normal."

Now and then, I looked at my friend and noticed the sadness that I had seen when we first met. Her emptiness seemed deeper than I could describe. I couldn't put my finger on it, but there was something about her. I sensed a deep void… I had never felt this from anyone before. We connected deeply; she was level-headed, and I loved her sense of humor. We talked for hours and spent the summer days relaxing in her backyard pool.

Her family was kind and accepting. Her mom was an amazing cook, and her dad was a hard worker and a good provider.

There were quiet moments when my friend and I were in the middle of deep conversation, sitting in her room or back in the pool; she'd begin a sentence, then suddenly stop halfway. She wanted to tell me something but never quite got to it.

One Sunday, she was getting something out of her closet. She suddenly turned to me and blurted, "I was going to ask you something, but I know you will say no."

"What? What do you want to ask me?" Finally, she is going to get to it, I thought.

"I was going to ask you if you wanted to go to church with my family."

Surprised, I said, "That's it? What's wrong with that? Yes, I want to go!"

Then she suddenly said, "Never mind, it's too late, next time." There was a conflict within her, which puzzled me; I didn't get it.

We continued to go out. To the beach, and the mountains and streams, hanging out in our swimsuits listening to music, and partying the summer away.

One day, their house phone rang, and her Mom said, "It's for Maria.

"For Me?" Who would know to find me here? It was my Dad, he had found me. "Hi, Dad." These words felt so familiar I had uttered them thousands of times. I was happy to be saying them. Holding back my tears, I wanted to say, "I miss you, Dad. Can I come home?"

But instead, I just listened quietly. "Look, Mija, (my daughter), I heard that you aren't with your boyfriend anymore, and I want to tell you that if you can promise me that you will behave, you can come home."

"Okay, Dad, I promise."

I was welcome home! My heart was overjoyed.

Just like that, I would be going home! My friend was curious and asked, "What did your Dad say?"

"He said I can come home," I answered quietly, wondering if I would be able to keep my word to my Dad. She seemed happy for me but a little sad that our summer together had come to an end; I certainly was. I made arrangements to leave that weekend, but I had made a friend for life.

I desperately needed direction for my life but didn't know where to get it. I was not aware that God pursues us. That he left us a whole book with instructions for life. A love letter straight from the heart of God.

"In all your ways, acknowledge him, and he will make straight your paths."

Proverbs 3:6. ESV

Chapter 25
You Can't Go Home Again

I have heard it said that you can't go home again.

I walked in through the door, and my siblings just looked at me and said, "Hey."

My Mom said, "Good, you are home." Our family didn't do well with displaying emotion." I could tell my Mom was very relieved.

I looked around, the same humble apartment, nice and clean. Same orange-brown, beige carpet. We joked and called it the "pizza-colored carpet" because it looked like pizza, and if you ever spilled on it, when returning with a rag to wipe it up, it was impossible to find the stain.

It felt strange to be home. I missed my family so much! However, when I got home, I didn't feel like I belonged there anymore. Their lives had moved forward without me in it. It felt like they were doing me a favor by allowing me to stay there. I felt a deep sadness as I realized this. "Home" for me didn't exist anymore.

Determined to keep my promise to my Dad, I hadn't let any of my friends know I was back, but somehow they found out.

Sitting awkwardly in the living room with my Dad and brother, I heard the house phone ringing in the other room.

"It's for you, Maria." my sister shouted. I picked up the receiver. "Hey, I heard you're back!" My friend said excitedly.

"Yup, I'm back."

"We're going to pick you up right now."

"Wait, no, I just got home." She was very persistent, so I asked my Dad, "Is it okay if my friend picks me up for a little while?" My Dad gave me a look of disappointment but didn't respond, and my mom looked worried.

One of my closest friends came and picked me up. Once in the car, I saw she wasn't alone. "We're going to another friend's house," she announced.

"But I told my dad I'd only be at your place for a little while," I protested. "I can't go."

"We're only going to be a little while; calm down," she said with a smile. Ignoring me, she continued driving. We arrived at our friend's house, where other friends were waiting, and of course, they had beer. I didn't want this, yet here I was again. I picked up right where I left off.

When I returned home later than I had promised, my Dad wouldn't even look at me. When I walked into a room, he walked out without a word. He was disappointed, and who could blame him? Why was I such a mess up?

I returned to school and decided to give it a good go.

I still tried to submerge the huge trauma "beach ball" under the turbulent waters. I still had no healing, and I still needed alcohol daily.

The curious thing was that when I was "homeless," staying with others, I felt unsafe, which caused me to draw firm boundaries for myself. I feared going beyond the point of no return. I could see it easily happen, I was in a precarious position. I put tight limits on what I would and wouldn't do. I didn't want to "lose it." beyond repair. But now that I was home and felt safe, I once again began to manifest the hidden trauma I was living with. It was still there, and I knew it.

As a result, I began partying again with friends, "Where's the party?" was our usual greeting. We'd all pack into our friend's van and head to other cities to party with guys we didn't know. We went to our first big concert, "The Isley Brothers, Rufus with Chaka Khan, Bootsy Collins and The Rubber-band Live," high on acid. I didn't't know what my friend handed me, I just obediently took it and spent the whole concert paranoid afraid I was going to fall onto the stage. "American Bandstand" was still going strong along with "Soul Train".

To only pay for one carload at the Drive-In we packed in tight sometimes even in the trunk. It was worth it to watch two movies and a cartoon at halftime, always hoping you wouldn't run into any enemies at the bathrooms or the concession stand.

We cruised in East LA down "The Boulevard" listening to oldies in someone's beautiful low-rider or went down to the Dam and hung out with all the "potheads" chillin' to Eric Clapton's "Baby I Love Your Ways". We danced to "Brick House", and "Boogie Nights", and were transfixed as we watched "Jaws" and "Grease". With all that endless activity, my heart was still broken, fun wasn't fixing things for me.

In those days, our social media was "the party line," which was a phone number you could dial (on the landline, of course), and all sorts of people would be on the line at the same time shouting out their names, their neighborhoods, or the parties going on. Many met potential dates on the party line. Everyone took turns with shout-outs. I could never talk when my friends would dial it up. I didn't have a cool thing to say; if I tried, I sounded like a teacher's aide just jumped on to check on the kids.

Meeting guys on here, driving down, and partying with complete strangers was not a safe idea. We weren't considering safety. It seems that danger does not compute well in a teenage mind. We met up with guys in their neighborhoods pretty regularly.

Neither my friends nor myself were from any gang, and "party" to us didn't mean sex. In our day, it simply meant dancing, drinking, and maybe some friends smoked marijuana. Occasionally, someone would make out with some guy they considered "cute."

It was still a risk. The girls from the neighborhoods we went to did not appreciate girls from other cities showing up and partying with their homeboys.

There were a few times when we narrowly escaped being killed.

At times, we found ourselves in very dangerous situations. Once, a guy from the neighborhood we were partying at had to get in our car and drive us out of the dead-end street. We had to sit in the back and duck down so we wouldn't be seen. The girls blocked the street and started shooting in our direction.

Bullets were flying, and chaos ensued. As the police chopper flew overhead, shining his light in our direction, the girls stopped him at the exit. He had to talk fast, trying to safely get us out of there. The girls were not having it; they were not letting him pass. The only thing that saved us was that he was well-respected in his neighborhood. These girls were not playing; they were serious about killing us.

On another occasion, we were partying in a house, drinking and smoking weed with these guys our friend knew.

At one point, I had to use the restroom. I walked down the hall, and as I opened the restroom door, I saw my friend semi-passed out, sitting on the floor, leaning on the tub. The guy she was with was trying to take advantage of her. "What are you doing!!" I began shouting at him. "Nothing, nothing, I wasn't doing nothing, man!" I was so angry! "YES YOU WERE!" I shouted, picking her up and walking her back to the living room.

I started pushing my friends, "Let's just leave. These guys are shady; let's go!" but I had a hard time convincing a few who were drunk. We had all gone there together in the van, so we had to leave together.

I noticed that my friends were also beginning to experience a downward spiral in their own lives. We were all going through the motions. We had lost the joy of life. Our conversations of hopes and dreams were now about how to bounce back from hurts and disappointment.

We all had broken hearts and now switched from thriving to merely existing. Most kept up with their schooling. However, when I spoke one-on-one with them, they shared the depth of their heartache and emptiness.

One day, while visiting a friend, she began to open up to me. "My boyfriend just left me for another girl." She was devastated. I felt it. Her eyes were lifeless, and her body language was one of total defeat.

I couldn't believe it. They were inseparable for a few years now. Her boyfriend drove a nice classic car, and she was always in the seat right next to him. Where you saw one, you saw the other. A prettier, more popular girl that he considered out of his league had given him the eye, and he dropped my friend in a hot second.

As she spoke, my once bubbly friend seemed to lose all her energy. She dabbed at her eyes trying to dry her tears. I suddenly realized that it was dark; we sat out in her yard on a picnic table talking as the sun went down. I wondered out loud, "Why do you wear that sweater in the summer heat?" She rolled her sleeve up and showed me her wrists. They were wrapped with a bandage. She had slit her wrists.

"We talked about our future together. He promised me the world. I had a miscarriage from him. I was over four months along in the pregnancy." Her words came out slowly, her face contorting with pain with every word.

She had given her boyfriend everything, and he just walked away. She could not bear the heartache. She spent her days sitting in a dark bedroom, wondering why she wasn't good enough for him.

"You are near, O Lord, And all Your commandments are truth." Psalms 145:18 NKJV

We were young and had been told by society that crossing all these moral boundaries was okay. They made it sound inconsequential, trivial. They asserted it would be "freedom," part of being young. They made it sound like fun and a full life!

We were, however, now reaping the consequences of crossing those moral boundaries. We bought into a lie that all these moral standards were outdated and set by old religious people trying to ruin our fun. The consequences were serious and devastating, no one was around to help pick up the pieces.

Some of their solutions only brought deeper trauma. "You are pregnant? Get rid of it. Add murder to your sexual immorality. Do you feel depressed because you ended your own baby's life? Deny that it was a human life, after all, it's your body, your choice..

Deny the reality of The Judeo-Christian God that is just out to ruin your fun. Follow a nonjudgmental god that you can make into your own image and adjust to your own convenience. You are now depressed? You have an eating disorder, you have a sexual addiction? You are cutting yourself? Do you have anxiety? Do some yoga, manifest what you want to see in your life, be positive. Let's not forget to put out good karma, and good energy, you can heal yourself. Your struggle has nothing to do with the fact that you deny the validity of The Bible. Just take care of Mother Earth, care for nature, and look to the universe. The universe will bring you what you need. "

Once you start on the road to denying The God of The Bible, you go down a slippery slope that sends you on a road of futility, an endless search.

Sex is more than a physical and emotional act. We are not simply animals that live from instinct and can mate with no spiritual attachment. We are spiritual beings. God gave us strict guidance for this powerful, beautiful act. It was meant to make one man and one woman one for life. Not to restrict and ruin our fun, but to protect and care for our body, soul, and spirit as the instruction manual instructs, and in doing so, avoid damage.

We have great value and need to handle our souls with care. When you give yourself in a sexual relationship, you become one and are joined to the other individual in the strongest, most significant way possible. If it is treated casually, you begin to see an emotional distortion of a once-healthy person. All sorts of issues arise, yet society refuses to connect them to the violation of biblical moral standards. Instead, they come up with a solution that exacerbates the harm. Then, a solution is found for the new trauma that was supposed to solve the first trauma, and you become more and more broken. Anything to maintain the rebellion against God, any other solution except the solution that acknowledges that God and the Bible are right.

God knows how He created us, He left us an instruction manual so that we would not misuse and corrupt our body, soul, and spirit.

Many young people have traveled this wide road that led to ruin and devastation. Some haven't made it out alive. I almost didn't. There are many more just now stepping onto this road. They've just started crossing boundaries and noted that nothing horrible happened. In fact, it was fun and enjoyable. These forbidden activities release so many endorphins that it is equivalent to the high you get from certain drugs, and you have become addicted. You reason maybe "religious" people are just trying to be restrictive and controlling.

How to convince them to listen? We didn't. How do we warn them that this pleasure that feels like freedom actually becomes bondage? Crossing these moral boundaries eventually enslaves us and damages our souls. How to encourage them to keep walking that straight and narrow road? Even when they are in the minority.

Pray for them, friend. Prayer to the God of the Bible is powerful and revolutionary. He will hear you, and He will respond!

And if it is you that is disregarding God's moral standards? Then reconsider your ways; they will not end well.

"Whoever heeds life-giving correction will be at home among the wise."
Proverbs 15: 31. NIV

"The path of life leads upward for the prudent to keep them from going down to the realm of the dead." Proverbs 15:24 NIV

The next day back in school after partying, my friend and I would talk about the amazing time we'd had the night before! We especially made a point to do this around other people and wanted them to believe we'd had so much fun partying. But it was a lie. We didn't, we didn't have a great time. Many of the places we went to were creepy, and the guys were no great catch. Everyone wore a facade and played this game portraying "I have a great life." But our reality was very different from what we let others see.

It is the same thing that is done on social media today. Everyone portrays their life as "awesome." There's a filter that smoothes out all the imperfections. When we spend our time looking at their perfect lives and compare it to our humdrum existence, we can get what I recently discovered has been labeled "FOMO," Fear Of Missing Out. Extreme depression and even suicidal tendencies are also connected to the overuse of social media.

My friends and I were all looking for something to fill our empty souls. We were searching for true love but were disappointed at every turn.

It was getting old, and we were going round and round on a hamster wheel and not getting anywhere.

I had seasons when I tried to change. I'd grown wary of the social charade and   determined that I was going to get my act together. I was going to get back to doing well in school. I loved learning. Even when I wasn't doing well, I loved watching educational programs. I watched documentaries and would keep my textbooks from school at the end of the year because I felt I had lost so much ground and had so much catching up to do. I would spend hours reading these textbooks in my room at home, secretly listening to country music. (Country music wasn't cool back then, and I would have lost many cool points if my friends found out.) Learning was energizing to me!

I also loved all music. I got a guitar and started attending night classes to learn guitar and voice lessons.

I was friends with an older lady who was an educator. She pulled some strings, so in addition to high school, I was accepted into a program to attend night school at ELAC. I started taking some college courses.

I had a few studious friends who encouraged me to pursue my education.

Although I loved my wild friends, I decided not to hang out with them.

I also worked as crowd control for The Los Angeles Convention Center and was able to listen at big-ticket events put on by respected philosophers, scientists, and intellectuals. This served to remove some of the mystique of Academia. I interacted with many of these VIPs and observed them off-stage when their guard was down. The term "book smart but not much wisdom" came to mind with some. I was very disappointed. I was searching! I had my eyes and ears peeled. I wanted to find meaning in this challenging existence.

These were some of the most intelligent people on the planet, and they definitely did not have the answers. I was losing my confidence in finding meaning in life. I figured this was it. Life disappoints, and I concluded there were no answers.

Let's note that I was still not okay; I was wounded, traumatized, and devastated and was merely coping. It took more and more energy to accomplish normalcy.

I could not fill the deep emptiness in my soul. I felt it all the time now, even more so when I stopped trying to mask it with alcohol. I was left with raw emotions that threatened to overwhelm me.

Outwardly, I was fighting and seemingly thriving; but inside, I was giving up. I felt lost, a fraud just playing the part. I knew what I wanted to do, but somehow, I always sabotaged my own success.

I had no way of repairing the internal damage already done.

I felt as though I had to proceed with care. I remember watching Western movies when I was small, where someone would get caught in quicksand. The more they struggled and thrashed around to get out, the deeper they sank. That's how I felt. My fight-or-flight instinct was always on high. How long would I be able to continue like this?

At times, I'd sit, and people watch, "normal people." How were they doing life so successfully? What was the secret? They were lucky to be born on the right side of the tracks, maybe? They must have all the resources they need. I concluded that they must be very intelligent and wise.

But every positive thought I had of them made me feel worse about myself until I was left feeling like a pitiful failure.

That familiar, sickening feeling in my gut gnawed at me and stole every ounce of self-worth. Sometimes, I felt invisible. Other times, I wished I could be.

I felt like a numb shell of a person that only contained pain and regrets. "I wish I could start life over," I whispered.

Chapter 26

You Are Pregnant

I eventually got back with my boyfriend, yes, the one who threatened my life with a knife. Not much that I did made sense.

I know this sounds repetitive, but I walked around with deep hopelessness, feeling I didn't belong anywhere. I also felt unworthy of love, even by my family. My boyfriend was just as wounded and insecure as I was. He didn't even know how to love himself. How could he show me love?

Many of my friends got pregnant and were having babies in high school. It wasn't rare to see a girl walking around with a large baby bump; it became so common that they had to create a "Teen Mother class and program."

I began to wish I could have a baby to have someone to love, someone who would never leave me. What an immature thought, right? I didn't factor in that babies grow up and babies have needs.

I see it now in hindsight, but then it was just another boundary removed. Another erroneous "way out".

I did get pregnant. This began to change my way of thinking, but not how I expected.

I suddenly began to see clearly how miserable and pointless my life was. This did not produce self-pity. Instead, it began to produce maturity.

How could I bring a child into this dysfunction? This baby became my "why". I began to open my eyes to my own responsibility to change my ways. I still had no tools to heal my addictions, trauma, pain, or anger. However, I felt responsible to do whatever it took to change things. I had seen how wealth, education, career, and relationships were good but not the answer. These things could enrich your life. However, they didn't get to the depth of your soul. I needed something that went deeper. I began to consider spirituality and truth. I had to find truth. I began to search in earnest.

I had friends telling me I was stupid and that I should "get rid of it." My boyfriend's life became absorbed by drugs, alcohol, and parties. He was getting his self-esteem from his reputation and the acceptance in his gang. He was moving up in rank.

So he became completely committed to it, and he started pulling on me to be that gangster girlfriend, but I wouldn't. I didn't want that life.

One day, I stopped by to talk to him. His Dad saw me pull up to their driveway, and he pulled me to the side, "You know that my son has no plans to quit doing his drugs, right?" He seemed tired and disappointed. "He is not good for you." He warned, "he is not going to change." He offered to pay for an abortion.

I understood he felt sorry for me and was only trying to help, but for me, an abortion was unthinkable. My response was,

"No, thank you, I can't do that." Even in my mixed-up way of thinking, I felt the seriousness of this decision.

I'm not saying this to throw anyone under the bus. I know he was looking out for me, but I thank God I was somehow already in love with the little one growing inside me.

Months later, after she was born, his parents would thank me, grateful that I had resolved not to abort.

My Dad didn't talk to me the whole time I was pregnant. I worried about how we would coexist in this small apartment. After I had given birth to her and brought her home, Mom and I walked into the bedroom and caught Dad by her crib, cooing and baby-talking to her. Both of our parents became grandparents for the first time through her, and she brought them so much joy. They loved her from the day they met her. I was glad that, for once, I had made the right choice.

That would happen later, but at this point, I didn't know what would happen. I was still overwhelmed. I was all set to be a statistic. I had not finished my education, had no support system, and was going to be a teen mother. I needed help, I needed a Savior… No one had introduced me to Him yet. So, all I had was a determination that I would not be broken.

I sat alone on my apartment stairs, thinking about my life. I was trying to take in the last of the soft, amber rays of the California setting sun, now quickly hiding over the second-story unit directly in front of mine. I softly whispered a prayer, "God, does everyone my age feel as trapped as I do?" It sure didn't seem that way.

Since around twelve years of age, I was often told how pretty I was. I could, however, never accept the compliments. I would look in the mirror, and all I saw were flaws. I felt awkward and stupid; I worried that these people who complimented me would one day look close enough and discover they were mistaken.

My life seemed dull and colorless, except for this baby growing inside me; I had no purpose. "How had my life come to this?" These were constant thoughts.

My family tried to raise me right. I tried to live right. But it didn't seem to matter. How did it all go so wrong? From day one, did I ever stand a chance?

What would I do with a baby? I'd continue staying in my parents' already overcrowded apartment. I would make it work somehow.

I was thinking about how I had dated a few decent, well-adjusted guys who were now planning their prospective colleges. One in particular tried hard to talk sense into me when I was at my darkest. I couldn't hear him, though. Instead, I chose to continue in the toxic relationship that shattered me and almost ended my life.

They seemed to know exactly where they were headed in life. I also knew at one time, how did it all go so wrong?

I smiled and acted confident and carefree, but I had the deepest void that nothing ever filled.

I had genuine friends, but they were just as lost as I was and were also acting. I was numb, and I didn't't seem to be able to feel true joy regardless of how hard I tried. I could, however, feel anger and rage. I could also feel regret, so much regret. My days and nights permeated with loneliness, fear, and anxiety.

Another whispered prayer, "God, how did I get here? Please help me."

My thoughts were interrupted by the echo of kids bouncing a ball in the long driveway. They were quickly headed to the fence that divided our apartments from the church next door. Someone had hit it with their car, and now there was no boundary between our apartments and the lighted church basketball court. Watching those kids reminded me that my life hadn't started this way. I remember being filled with hope for the future and excitement for the possibilities of what I would become one day.

Don't get me wrong, I'd had some trauma, but in those days of innocence, I was able to bury it and move forward.

Back then, I had tenacity and determination to live a good life. I believed that God existed; therefore, good existed. The world felt safe.

The memories came flooding back. Memories of my early teen years. How I found joy in walking to the community pool with friends on a hot summer day. Later, on the way back home, still in our wet swimsuits and flip-flops, darker by multiple shades than we had been when we walked to the pool earlier that day. We'd stop at the Circle K to buy a "big stick" ice cream, a bag of sunflower seeds, a pickle, and a Coke; such fun!

Back then, I celebrated my good grades and the fact that schoolwork was not difficult for me at all. I loved music even then, and much to my older brother's dismay, I also loved singing. I would purchase lyric books to the latest songs that had just come out and sing them all at the top of my lungs, imagining that I was the original artist.

I also loved dancing in my dance group, Ballet Folklorico, in Jr. High; we traveled to other cities, performing at park kiosks and halls. I loved it. We wore beautiful regional costumes, I loved the beauty of twirling to the rhythm of the mariachi. The yards and yards of colorful ribbon and fabric resembled flowers in full bloom.

I believed my future was bright if I applied myself, kept my nose clean, and worked hard. I truly tried. I was studious, tried to mind my parents, and revered the God I'd learned about in my Mom's church, but somehow my life still lost its color.

My pregnancy took away the option of giving up on life. I had a mother's instinct to protect my baby. The fact that I had so little to offer her saddened me deeply. I exhaled with deep exhaustion, my brain going around and around, attempting to find peace.

I still needed to drink, especially when things went wrong, but I did my best not to. Was it a problem? Why couldn't I completely stop thinking of alcohol? Had I become an alcoholic? These thoughts haunted me. I constantly thought about how I'd be able to drink again after my baby. I felt my conscience prod me; I was sending prayers up more often now. I wondered if I was praying right.

I wasn't sure of the correct delivery that would bring the right results. My search for truth was constant now. It became a search for God.

Any religion that showed up at my door was welcome to come in. I'd sit and listen to Jehovah's Witnesses, Mormons, and anyone who would tell me about God. I also attended the church I was raised in. I participated and listened intently but left the same. The words never quite reached the depth of my soul.

I began to develop resentment at this elusive God who didn't care to answer me.

One day, two young men came to my house and explained their religion to me. I had sat and listened patiently with an open heart. I prayed a prayer with them and felt a strange peace. The young men knew I was feeling this peace and said, "You know how you know this religion is true?"

"How?" I answered.

"By the way you are feeling now," he said.

I was a bit spooked that they knew how I was feeling and thought, "Maybe this is the way." However, there was something off with how I felt.

Years later, I realized that this peace reminded me of the "soothing feeling" I had when attempting suicide.

After the young men left, I immediately went to the room, knelt, and, feeling a bit hopeful, prayed the same prayer again.

I said, "God, I'm going to repeat that prayer. Let me feel that peace again if this is the right way." I prayed, but instead of peace, I felt a cold, clammy feeling. This made me angry. "God, I don't believe in you. You are not real!" The letdown felt exaggerated.

"You don't exist; if you do exist, you are not good! Because here I am calling out to you in desperation, can't you see me? I'm hurting. I want to know you! Why don't you answer?" I felt the tears coming, but I didn't allow myself to cry. I felt my heart harden. "You don't care! "Answer me!" I challenged Him angrily.

I collapsed in bed, exhausted. Angry tears ran down my face into my ears as I cried in disappointment.

The sun rose, and my eyes opened to another day, just another day. I was deeply saddened every second, every minute of every hour.

I was on a search for peace, for truth, for meaning.

I blamed God for all the hardship and misery in my life. I wasn't considering that real evil exists in this world, working to steal, kill, and destroy life. Neither was I considering the human element. Our decisions affect our lives and the lives of others.

God was not the author of my misery. He was working overtime behind the scenes to draw me. In this world of free will, I had to come to him out of my own free will. However, he is God and doesn't adjust or change the truth to avoid offending us. He is truth, and we must come to truth in surrender, accepting his whole truth. He is God; he does not change, and for that, we should be grateful. This attribute is what makes him completely reliable, always. It is not just ANY truth that sets us free, It is His truth that sets us free.

"For I am the Lord, and I do not change; That is why your descendants of Jacob are not destroyed" Malachi 3: 6 NLT

"Jesus Christ is the same yesterday, today, and forever." Hebrews 13:8 KJV

One day, all my mess would work for my good because he is the God who saw me and heard me. However, on this day, and at this moment, I didn't know this. I was angry and flailing in the dark, not realizing I wasn't far from the encounter of a lifetime!

"And we know that for those who love God, all things work together for good, for those who are called according to his purpose. For those whom he foreknew, he also predestined to be conformed to the image of his Son so that he might be the firstborn among many brothers". - Romans 8:28-29 ESV

My senses were elevated. Everywhere I went, my search continued; I looked for any hint of truth, any hint of God. Whenever I hung out with friends, which was happening less and less, I observed married couples who at one time may have been deeply in love yet now seemed trapped and unhappy.

One evening, a few friends and I sat in our friend Sandy's living room. All with drinks in hand, music playing softly, and toddlers playing on the floor. Sandy received a call and then returned, looking upset. She pulled me aside and asked me, "Will you go with me to the bar? I need to go see if my husband is there," she added quietly, "with another woman."

I agreed to go. Baby on hip, she grabbed her keys. She got behind the wheel and handed me her baby, who I sat on my lap. It was dark in her van, but I could see her eyes as she spoke nervously. Wide-eyed, she confided, "He does this often; he doesn't even come home after work." I felt her pain. She parked in front of the bar and picked up her baby, who, seeing her exit the car, had begun crying. "I'll be right back."

I watched her go into the bar, baby in tow, and my mind went back to when I first met them. This was a relationship that others envied. They had seemed like the perfect match. She said nothing but was visibly upset when she came back. Her baby was red and whimpering.

"He was in there with some chick; he didn't even try to hide it!" she finally said and seemed too angry to cry. "I told him to come home; he said he'll get there when he gets there." She hammered the steering wheel with her clenched fist, startling her baby, who again began to cry.

Misery surrounded me. "Was it always there, or am I just now seeing it?"

I watched professionals, relatives, and friends from various economic and educational levels. They all seemed to be running a race of futility. I observed them all closely and began to lose heart. A meaningful life seemed an elusive myth.

My friends still planned parties, gathered to drink, meet up with guys, and "have fun." Only it wasn't fun, and I was no longer pretending it was.

Some friends mentioned that I seemed different. I seemed gloomy all the time.

I didn't realize this then, but God was opening up my eyes to see the true condition of my surroundings. He was setting me up for an encounter with Truth, an encounter with Him.

Some of my older friends continued their education, and some started great careers. Still, to my disappointment, they expressed the same weariness and sense of futility. Whenever we engaged in real and transparent conversations, the mask came off. In the end, they were left as empty as before.

Days bled one into another, and I dreaded each one. My determination to improve for the little soul inside me was the only thing keeping me moving forward. I wanted to do right by my child, yet it was a glaring fact that I needed "saving" myself. I was so lost.

Chapter 27
My Appointment
A Beautiful Exchange!

After school, a few friends and I sat around. As usual, one said," I'm bored; where's the party?" Never mind that it was a weekday. Another friend added, "Let's do something".

"What is there to do?" I asked.

The friend whose house we were at piped up, "My aunt invited me to a Rally." I instantly thought, "Pep Rally," football or some other sport came to mind. "Let's go," I said.

A few other friends agreed, and around five of us packed into my friend's car and headed for this "Rally." We arrived at the address. It was a park, but there was no activity outside. "Isn't that where rallies are held? Outside?" It was raining cats and dogs, and the wind blew so strongly that it made it difficult to open the car door. I thought, "Only crazy people would be out in this weather!

And yet here we were, my crazy group of friends and a small group from a church meeting inside the community center, holding a "Jesus Rally." We didn't know that it was a church thing yet.

I exited my friend's car, and the wind blew my long coat, making it hard to tie the belt to close it. I put my hood on and leaned into the wind, trying to see our surroundings through the rain. We heard someone shouting, "Over here!"

A young man had seen us through the glass double doors, stepped out, and began to wave us in. "Over here!"

We walked into the reception area, and he directed us to a small room they had rented for the occasion.

My friends and I walked through the double doors in the small hall. Something instantly hit me; it was an overwhelming feeling I had never felt before. I began to weep, but these tears were different. They were the tears a child cries when lost, and they had to be brave. Then, after a long while of trying to find their way, they spot Mom or Dad, and tears begin to pour out of their eyes as they fall into Mom/ and Dad's embrace.

I quickly made it to a chair, where about 20 others were sitting. I had never seen nor felt such a thing. The band in front of the room played songs I had never heard. There was a strong presence, something holy permeating the entire hall. The songs were about Jesus.

After each song, someone was called out from the small crowd. They walked up to the mic and boldly shared about the darkness their life had been and the incredible transformation that had taken place in them once they surrendered to Jesus. They exuded freedom! Could this be true? Could this be real? The presence I felt was awe-inspiring. It felt like a hurricane of truth hitting me all at once.

I could not stop my tears, "What is happening to me? How embarrassing!" A child was sitting next to me. I didn't know who this child belonged to, but I put him on my lap to hide that I was crying uncontrollably. What was this overwhelming presence? It was holy! What was happening to me? Why was I crying, and why could I not stop?

I wasn't catching what was being said or even the song lyrics. I couldn't focus because this strong presence had captivated me. There was a special atmosphere that I could visibly see and feel. Could this be God?

I encountered His precious Holy Spirit that day. I had challenged Him, and He had answered! Oh MY, this was overwhelming. I sensed His majesty, His holiness, His power! It was all indescribable. Whoa, this was not a lightweight, mediocre God that I could hurl accusations at. His majesty became real to me. How dare I speak to Him the way that I had, and how humble of Him to take the insults and still continue to pursue me.

However, more than anything, I felt his love. It was a different kind of love. Gentle, kind, and overwhelming, it covered me like a heavy blanket.

Then, the next thing I knew, I rose from my seat uninvited and made my way to the front of the room. There had been no invitation to come forward yet. (I had never seen an altar call; this wasn't done in the church I grew up in.) The sense that I stood before His Majesty and Holiness made my knees buckle and shake; I felt that I may just fall on my knees.

I was upfront by myself and suddenly became self-conscious. "What am I doing up here?" I thought, "Maybe I'm having a nervous breakdown." I was about to turn to walk back to my seat, but a young lady came up behind me and asked, "Can I pray for you?"

"YES!" I answered.

I closed my eyes as she led me in a prayer of repentance. I repeated after her, "Jesus, forgive me for all my sins, come into my life, and be my Lord and my Savior; I will serve you from this day forward."

WOW! I felt like the dark kingdoms in my heart were slowly dismantled; I sensed chains breaking, fog lifting, filth being washed clean.

I felt the power of almighty God! It was an encounter with Truth, and I bowed in surrender!

I opened my eyes and realized I had been the first of many who had walked up to receive Christ that day. My eyes were filled with happy tears.

The young lady who prayed for me invited me to a side room, and I followed her. The others who had received Christ were also there.

She began to read the scriptures to me and explain that I was now "born again." I was a "new creation in Christ Jesus," forgiven of all my sins and washed clean.

Something unexpected began to happen to me as she spoke. I became hot, and rage built up inside my gut; anger began to overwhelm me. I could not make eye contact with the young lady who was speaking to me.

I became restless and sweaty. I was highly irritated, and a voice inside me began screaming angrily, "Don't listen to her! Tell her to shut up! Tell her to shut up! Don't listen to her! Run, Run, Run!" I began to breathe heavily as you do after a quick sprint. She was unaware of what was happening inside me or the battle I was fighting. She patiently continued to explain salvation to me.

"If you know where the restroom is, please take me; I'm about to throw up," I broke in and pleaded suddenly.

Looking at me, a bit puzzled, she noticed I didn't look well, grabbed me by the hand, and we ran to the restroom which was all the way on the opposite side of the facility.

When we arrived, she stood back and watched, bewildered, as I began to heave and vomit into the sink. Only it wasn't vomit; it looked more like black foam. It quickly dissolved into the drain; then again, I would begin to heave and gag. I felt a resistance; something refused to come out, and then I'd finally vomit again into the sink. The same black foam would come up and dissolve quickly into the sink.

It happened to me five times, and then, on the sixth time, it was a bit harder. This one did not want to leave! I felt extremely strong resistance, but everything within me wanted it gone! I was a brand new person; this thing did not belong inside me anymore. It was causing me more strain, but finally, it all came out! My eyelashes had fallen off into the sink, but I didn't care; I felt brand new! I felt light; the burden was gone! I felt clean, I felt free! WOW!

I looked at the bathroom ceiling and exclaimed, "What a beautiful bathroom!" Then I looked at the sweet young lady who had led me to Christ and said, "This is the first time I can look you in the eyes!"

I said, "I feel like all the bad stuff inside me just came out." She looked back at me wide-eyed and said slowly, "Yes, I think it has."

I had no paradigm for what just happened to me but had no doubt that I had just encountered the living God, and no one could ever convince me otherwise!

That day I was delivered from all the demons that had me bound back to the day I had tried to kill myself and probably back to the date rape, maybe even further back. Jesus set me free! He came in, and they came out! I did not want that life anymore. I could not express with words how wonderful I felt!

Jesus is mighty, He is good, and He is unwilling that any should perish, but He wants all to come to repentance. Repentance is a good thing; it is a positive thing. Like shedding all the weight that holds us back, washing all the filth, breaking every chain! He desires to change our minds and turn our lives around.

He is holy and cannot embrace sin, so he made a way for our sins to be washed clean.

It becomes our choice. We can forsake sin and embrace God, or we can forsake God and embrace sin. However, we cannot have it both ways. It is entirely up to us.

That day, I embraced God and determined to forsake sin.

I went into that little community center, one hopeless, miserable, lost, confused person. I walked out a whole, brand-new creation, forgiven and cleansed. I was not the same. I felt it. I knew God had answered my challenge! He had responded to my prayer. I had been made new!

"For I know the plans I have for you, declares the Lord, plans for welfare and not for evil, to give you a future and hope. Then you will call upon me and come and pray to me, and I will hear you. You will seek me and find me when you seek me with all your heart. I will be found by you, declares the Lord, and I will restore your fortunes and gather you from all the nations ..."
Jeremiah 29:11-14 NIV

Ch*apter 28*

MOM, I HAVE BEEN SAVED!

When I got home, I told everyone in the house about this new birth that I had experienced! My Mom was upset with me because I had gone to the rally without telling her, so once again, not knowing my whereabouts, she was worried for me. "Mom, I gave my heart to Jesus! I am born again, I am forgiven!"

She was so over me and my drama. She got mad at me because I "changed religions" and didn't want to hear it, and she didn't want me putting this "nonsense" in my sibling's head.

I had been instantly delivered from my pack-a-day cigarette habit; I had no more compulsion to drink. I woke up the next day hearing the birds singing; I could breathe, my soul felt light, and the unbearable heaviness was gone.

Wow! I found the reason for living! I found the meaning of life. I found God, or should I say, God found me! Jesus became my everything; I was in awe of Him.

I attended a party that same weekend that I received Christ (I didn't know Christians don't attend these parties). I thought, "I will not indulge heavily; I can maintain." I tried to drink, but I remained completely sober no matter what I drank. It was a disco party; people danced around the pool on an elevated outdoor patio, colored strobe lights flashing. I was a little confused about what was happening to me. Why wasn't I enjoying myself? I literally could see the puppet masters that were moving all these individuals.

A friend showed me some rolled-up blunts and asked me to go outside. This was strange because it was a friend who had become addicted and never shared any of her drugs, yet here she was, offering to share. The devil did not want to let go of me; he wanted to entrap me again. I was ignorant of this fact.

I followed her, thinking, "Well, since the alcohol hasn't affected me, maybe I can catch a buzz with some weed." My flesh was alive and trying to get me to return to sin. Marijuana wasn't even my drug of choice. The devil was working overtime, trying to draw me back.

I was about to smoke with her, but when she lit the blunt, the familiar "angel dust" chemically smell filled the air. I never even touched it. Just then, My other friend's boyfriend drove up, got out of his car, and began to beat her for being at a party without him. He was pounding her as if he was hitting a guy! Then his older brother saw him and began to beat him, telling him, "Leave her alone," but her boyfriend would not let go of her hair, so she was getting trampled. He was bloody, she was bloody, and her hair was a tangled mess, full of grass. They shouted at one another, cursing and threatening!

Everyone from the party came running out to see the fight.

My boyfriend had also come with my friend's boyfriend, neither of us had told them we would be there. However, although he wouldn't beat me, he was demanding, "What are you doing here?"

Just then, I heard a voice clearly say, "Maria, you don't belong here anymore!" I recognized the voice. It was God. I instantly knew this was Holy Spirit. I recognized that I was hearing His truth.

Everyone from the party was standing up on the curb, so I got on the street directly in front of them and began to tell them, "The day before yesterday, I gave my life to Jesus; he has set me free, and I am going to follow him, I don't belong here anymore, from now on I'm going to church. If any of you ever want to know about Jesus, give me a call, and I will tell you where my church is." (Never mind that I had not gone to the church yet, but I knew the girl who prayed with me at the rally would pick me up on Sunday.) I told them, "You will never see me back here again; I am going to follow Jesus."

It was true; I didn't belong there anymore. I told my boyfriend, "I gave my life to Jesus, and I'm going to go to church from now on. If you want to follow Him with me, you are welcome; if not, this is goodbye because I am never returning to this life again."

He looked at me as if I had lost my mind and said, "You are tripping; you'll be back."

I realized that I had my answer from him. I turned and walked away, alone, but I was not alone. As I walked down the dark street, I could hear the music and the voices fading. No one followed me, but I was at peace, finally, after so many years.

I would never, ever be alone again.

I made it to the liquor store phone booth and dialed up Mom, "Mom, can you pick me up?" Mom was accustomed to constant drama in my life, "Are you okay?" she asked with a worried edge in her voice. "I'm okay, Mom."

She found me sitting on the curb, and I saw her puzzled, concerned look. "I'm fine, Mom," I said softly.

I grew up that day. I also grew brave; I had a courage that surprised even me. I was just 17. It was January 1979. The year had just begun, and I had just started to live truly!

On November 18, 1978, Peoples Temple founder Jim Jones led hundreds of his followers in a mass murder-suicide at their commune in a remote part of Guyana. Many of Jones' followers willingly ingested a poison-laced punch, while others were forced to do so at gunpoint. The final death toll at Jonestown that day was 909; a third of those who perished were children. In the mind of my friends and family, Jim Jones was a "Christian" Pastor.

Two months later, around January 18th, I walked into that community center and encountered The living God, who set me free and would radically transform my life.

Family members and friends warned me strongly against the dangers of becoming a Christian. They said my Pastor was probably another Jim Jones. Whenever I shared the salvation message, they would say that I had "drank the Cool-Aid." However, my encounter with Christ was so real and revolutionary that none of these things moved me. I had found the truth, and nothing would dissuade me from following Jesus!

I lost all my friends that day, my family thought I was crazy, I was an unwed, pregnant teenager just finishing high school, I had no car of my own, and I lived with my parents in a run-down apartment. I didn't know how I would make ends meet when my baby came.

But I didn't care; the inside of my soul was healed and whole! I felt that I could face whatever came my way. Jesus was with me.

That young lady and her husband from the rally picked me up for church on Sunday, Wednesday, and Friday. Thursday Bible Studies, then Saturday outreach. Telling others who, like me, found themselves lost and hopeless about this loving Savior Jesus became my passion. I was home, loved by Jesus, and I loved learning about my new faith.

I did whatever I had to do to get to church. My friend and his sister gave their lives to Jesus. Their dad owned an ice cream truck; when we needed a ride to church, we'd empty the ice cream truck of the freezers, load the truck with people standing (as there were no seats), and head over to church in the noisy truck! Anything to get there.

Once, I knocked on a long-time neighbor's door; he didn't know me. I had never spoken to him or his family before, but I had invited a friend to church that day, and we needed a ride. He looked at me like I was crazy, but he gave us a ride, and when we arrived in the church parking lot, I testified passionately about

Jesus and invited him to come in for service. He refused but said, "If you ever need a ride to your church, just ask."

I didn't know much, but I knew that once I was dead in my sin, and now I was alive in Christ, and that is precisely what I shared.

"Giving thanks to the Father… 13Who has delivered us from the power of darkness, and has translated us into the kingdom of his dear Son: 14 In whom we have redemption through his blood, even the forgiveness of sins: Colossians 1:12-14.

"And you, that were sometime alienated and enemies in your mind by wicked works, yet now has he reconciled." - Colossians 1:21 KJV

Chapter 29

My Little Red New Testament Revealed

I remembered the red New Testament that I was given in 5th grade by Mr. Coughlin; many years had passed, I'd moved, and Middle school, with its silly games, became a distant memory.

Throughout the years, many times, I'd be cleaning out my dresser drawers and find my red New Testament, and remembering the promise I had made Mr. Coughlin, I would crack it open, 'cross myself, focus, and try my best to read it… and NOTHING. I never understood it. I always had my Mom's words in the back of my mind, "It's not a real Bible." I grew to believe that she was right; the only reason I kept it was because of the promise I had made Mr. Coughlin.

Then, I lived through family crises and the high school years, trying to maneuver life with a grown-up body but a child's brain: a date rape, a suicide attempt at 15. An angry young woman would open that red New Testament and … still NOTHING. I had thrown my red New Testament away numerous times after being unable to understand it. Once, I even threw it in the big, green dumpster. But Mr. Coughlin and the promise I made him would pull at my conscience, and I would find myself digging through the trash to retrieve my red New Testament. I'd carefully clean the cover and put it safely in a drawer.

Then, that fateful day that I got radically, undeniably saved, after a few weeks of this new life, one day while cleaning out my drawer, I once again found and immediately opened my red New Testament.

Wow! The words leaped out at me; they made my heart race. I felt a stirring inside me as I read and devoured the words on the page! They made sense, and I was overjoyed.

I now know that *"The Gospel is foolishness to those who perish, but unto us who are being saved, it is the power of God unto salvation."* 1 Cor. 1:18.

I now understand that *"The carnal mind cannot comprehend the things of the Spirit, for they are spiritually discerned."* 1Cor. 2:14

The Bible speaks my new language! I do not doubt that Mr. Coughlin prayed for me. He planted the seed that changed my life. I cannot wait to see him in heaven and thank him for my red New Testament.

My new life was not suddenly easy. In fact, it was very complicated, but I had Jesus, and I was not going to give him up for anything the world had to offer. I was not going to return to my vomit. Harsh words, but that is how the Bible describes our sinful life before Christ. I did not want ever to go back there; it wasn't worth it.

I chose to search His Word aggressively and to speak His Word faithfully. I chose to declare His Word boldly and stubbornly stand on His truth! Church became my second home, I absolutely loved attending and serving at my church.

As a result, I began to see a transformation in my heart, then in my speech, then in my LIFE!

I had my baby six months into my new life as a Christian. She has never seen her Mom living that wild life of sin. As a new believer in those early months and years, I prayed, "Lord, bring me a man of God who will love my daughter as his own flesh and blood." I refused to be happy at her expense.

God blessed me with an incredible Man of God whom I met and married in the church. This man has loved my daughter as his very own. We then had two more beautiful girls.

My husband Clemente and I dedicated our life to serving in our church. We mentored other couples. We cleaned the church, worked the nursery, ushered in the parking lot, picked people up for church, taught Bible Studies, and anything else needed.

We studied the word and doctrine, but what was significantly transforming was the personal accountability and character training. Nine years into my life in Christ, we were ordained. My husband and I and our daughters, Andrea, Alena, and Adelle, moved to Orange County to establish a new church plant in Placentia, CA. We are not giving people religion; religion doesn't work, we give people Jesus.

We've had the joy of bringing many to know Christ, the life-giver, and seeing their lives transformed.

The Lord directed us to take a challenging church in Pasadena that needed some restoration. This was our second pastorate. We were very fruitful there and loved that beautiful congregation.

After four years, God called us out to the deep again and, in 1991, challenged us to St. Petersburg, Russia. A country with a collapsed economy at the time. We didn't know the language or anyone there but knew we heard God. What a privilege to preach the gospel of Jesus Christ in a country that had been atheist for over 70 years!

When we married, my husband and I had agreed, "Whatever God says, wherever he sends us, we will never tell him no. He has our yes."

So we sold or gave away all our belongings except what could fit in two suitcases per family member, we said goodbye to our extended family, we said goodbye to our beautiful church, we said goodbye to The United States of America, and off we flew to live in the former Soviet Union, to share the hope that had transformed our lives. We found that the Gospel works everywhere, even in Russia!

That story deserves its own book, but besides building a precious church filled with beautiful Russian people, we also became pregnant there after nine years of believing that the baby shop was closed.

The American Embassy informed us of the high infant mortality rate at the time and warned us against giving birth in Russia. After researching different alternatives, we had no option but to return to America.

So, we returned home at six and one-half months along in the pregnancy. We were blessed with our first and only boy,

Joshua Brandon, and we also took a pastorate in a small church in the city of Montebello, which, once again, God blessed and made very fruitful.

Some years later, while in this thriving church, we were again challenged to go to another Eastern European Country, Tallinn, Estonia. We left our eldest daughter here in the States with my Mom. She had graduated, ready for college, and had found good employment. We knew it was time for her to begin building her own life, and she remained here in America. With a broken heart, and with our two teenage daughters and two-year-old son, we boarded a plane to the Country of Estonia.

We returned from Estonia and went to the beautiful city of San Diego, CA, where we once again pioneered a new church plant. This church was exceptionally fruitful. We were privileged to witness Jesus revolutionize lives in the best way possible as the most broken of society surrendered their heart to Christ. We later found out that the gang we were reaching out to and seeing revival break out in had murdered the Pastor that had been there before us. A fact that we were glad to be ignorant of at the time. God gave us many souls in San Diego!

After seven years, we were again challenged to take another church going through a difficult time. We had pastored them before and knew and loved them dearly, so we dropped everything and went ready to see God do his thing there in restoring this church. We believed for great things and poured our life out for them.

After 17 years there, we once again left a thriving church and, at the writing of this book, are presently pioneering our 8th

Pastorate Remnant Church WestCo—a new work in the City of West Covina, CA. We opened the church in the heat of Covid. It was a challenge, but God is faithful, and we are excited for what God has in store for us!

We don't view pastoring as a career but a calling. We count it a privilege to be involved in God's great mission to rescue the broken and the lost. Each church mentioned above represents numerous lives restored one at a time. The message of salvation was communicated to them, and they chose to say yes to Jesus. We are simply the messengers, sent with the most important message you will ever hear.

Jesus loves you; he took your sin and nailed it to the cross, and if you take him as Lord and Savior, If you live your life for him, he will give you a better life now, and eternal life will follow. What a beautiful exchange!

God has been faithful to us. He's given us the highest purpose in life. Our life is not our own; we are His ambassadors. Our feet have touched foreign soil, and we've preached His message of freedom and redemption in many countries and continents, as well as in back alleys and crime-ridden, depressed neighborhoods here in the US. We also host our Television program Unstoppable Broadcasting on HSBN international in Spanish and English on 25 platforms, to 190 countries from five to seven million viewers. We were presented with our Doctorate of Divinity in 2020 and want to make our lives count for His glory bringing His light to this darkened world. He has our YES!

Our greatest treasure is our family and our legacy. Our children have also sacrificed so much and been a great support in every church we've pastored.

Our daughter Andrea, my motivation in those early, dark years to search for truth, has been such a beautiful, godly example and has blessed us with two handsome grandsons, Tyler and Cayden, who are now teenagers.

Our sweet daughter Alena and her husband Michael care for my husband and me and "watch our back." Our Adelle has always been supportive, hard-working, responsible, and the life of the party, the crazy fun to our family.

Our hard-working son Josh is a godly father and husband, a talented musician, and a teacher of The Word. He and his beautiful bride Kim are worshippers and have blessed us with the cutest grandchildren, JB, Emery, and Silas, whom we love dearly! They all love Jesus, and we are grateful for what God still has planned for each one of them. What a gracious, and generous God.

He is calling you as well; he desires to change your life. You may have everything going for you, but if you don't have Jesus, you are not equipped for the spiritual battles you will doubtless face.

He wants to take your sin and give you his righteousness.

He was rejected so that you would be accepted; He suffered stripes upon his back so that you may have healing. He took your poverty so that you could become a co-heir with him. He was declared guilty so that you would be declared innocent. He was forsaken so that you would be loved. The Father turned his face from him so that He could behold your face forever. Jesus loves you!

What a beautiful exchange!

"For God so loved the world (that means YOU) that He gave His one and only Son, that everyone who believes in Him shall not perish but have eternal life. 17 For God did not send His Son into the world to condemn the world, but to save the world through Him." John 3:16-17 NIV

WHAT OTHERS ARE SAYING

"The author of this book is far more than just an acquaintance of mine. Maria has been a dedicated fellow laborer in Christ within a collaborative fellowship of churches for numerous years. Her journey serves as a beacon of hope for those familiar with the depths of inner struggles. Through her story, one witnesses the profound impact of encountering Jesus and cultivating a steadfast faith, pointing the way to overcome adversities.

Within these pages, you'll embark on a journey toward understanding what it truly means to triumph in Christ. The narrative unfolds, revealing the resilience of the human spirit against the trials that seek to darken and destroy the soul. You'll find nuggets of wisdom and insight, guiding you along a path of faith, hope, and eventual victory.

This book extends an invitation to believe in a compassionate God who deeply cares for all, especially those who feel unworthy of His love. Through the author's experiences, you'll be inspired and emboldened to confront life's greatest challenges. Even in the darkest moments, the light of Christ shines, offering redemption and restoration.

More than a mere tale, this book serves as a powerful testament to human resilience, empowered by the boundless grace of a loving God. It encourages you to confront your own trials with unwavering faith, patience, and reliance on divine strength. Prepare to be deeply moved, inspired, and transformed as you journey alongside the author towards a life illuminated by hope, purpose, and steadfast faith."

Dr. Edwin Melendez
Lead Pastor of Culture City Church
Cicero Illinois

"For the last 12 years, we have been both influenced and inspired by the incredible testimony of Maria Casas. Her life has been a flame of light for God and a target for the devil. At a young age she was confronted with a darkness that no child should ever experience, but God has traded His beauty for her ashes. Instead of becoming a statistic, she surrendered to the leading of Jesus Christ and her life has been used to rescue thousands of people from darkness. A BEAUTIFUL EXCHANGE draws us in with authentic and compelling storytelling painting vivid pictures of the characters and circumstances that formed Maria's life experience. Simultaneously, it teaches us critical life lessons out of the human experience – mind, body, and spirit.

A BEAUTIFUL EXCHANGE sheds light on how God not only loves us but wants to navigate our lives at every stage. There is a powerful heavenly realm that surrounds us, and a demonic realm that takes cheap shots when we don't know, or we forget our place as a child of God. In this powerful retelling, Maria exposes the enemy and his predictable tactics attempting to steal, kill and destroy our promises, purposes and very lives. Most importantly, she teaches us how to face the darkness, protect ourselves and our loved ones, then defeat our foes.

No matter where we find ourselves in life, A BEAUTIFUL EXCHANGE points out a separate unseen truth that is more important than what we can see. Maria's journey exemplifies Proverbs 3: 5-6, "Trust in the Lord with all your heart, and lean not on your own understanding; in all your ways acknowledge him, and He will direct your paths."

As you turn each page keep your heart and mind open to revisiting moments in your own life to receive new understanding and revelation. Be prepared to make a fruitful exchange of beauty for ashes, strength for fear, joy for mourning, peace for despair, and freedom for captivity."

Trey & Ariel Fernald
Co-Founders of Eastern Sky Theatre Company
Authors of "Producing Drama for Ministry"

"I've had the privilege of knowing Maria Casas for 30 years. During this time I've seen how God has used her wherever she's been in ministry alongside of her husband, Clem.

In the years that Maria has been in ministry, she has helped countless women come into the emotional and spiritual healing power of Jesus Christ. God has demonstrated to Maria that she is a treasure that came out of darkness (Isaiah 45:3). Maria's revelation of this Biblical truth has been used of God as an instrument to God's restorative power.

I am convinced that this book will be a platform for God to reach many people who have experienced deep, emotional pain and trauma, and convey His love and grace in transforming their lives. Maria's book will lead you in a journey of finding the love and grace of God in your life. "

Mrs. Sara Torres
Senior Pastors' wife
Legacy Church Salinas

"This book is like a multifaceted diamond. It exposes the enemy in so many different ways! Pastor Maria pulls the covers off the spirit of suicide, so it is exposed! Through her life story, she teaches the tactics of the enemy and how to break free with the Word of God! In her journey you see the power of God transform her life! Pastor Maria shows you through the Word of God how to equip yourself to fulfill your destiny."

Dr. Vanisia Tapia
Founder of Sustaining Fire Ministries

"A good story can draw you in and begin to reach you without you even realizing it. In this liberating book, you'll be taken on a journey of innocence and hope, then witness how the unseen spiritual realities around her affect and influence her to the point of teenage folly and self-destruction. She shares wisdom and truth gained in the struggle for survival from the hopelessness and confusion of youth. The struggle with alcohol, teen pregnancy, depression, abuse.

While you learn how to identify the root of your anger, stress, depression, and disappointment. Dr. Maria Casas shares that there is an answer to a life of turmoil. Peace is achievable even when everything around you seems out of control. You don't have to live on the defense as if you're always carrying a white flag ready to surrender to your circumstances. NO!!!

This book will help you rise above, and see through adverse situations, and even the wrongful actions of others. But most importantly, it will reveal how you can come out of spiritual darkness into a joyous fellowship with Christ as "an overcomer" in life. I wholeheartedly recommend this great message of encouragement.

The words within this book are God's Revelation to you for healing, deliverance, and salvation. The devil tried his best to destroy her and to permanently silence her voice, he failed! It is now her mission and purpose to educate and equip you through this impactful message of hope, comfort, and faith. Additionally, this message was designed to help you get into God's presence, understand who you are in Christ, find significance and personal value, break the bonds of demoniac influence, FOR GOD HAS CALLED YOU TO GREATNESS! Finally remember, that Jesus Christ is no respecter of persons, what he did for Dr. Maria, He will do for YOU!… The devil is still a liar and loser… GOD'S WORD STILL WORKS... YOU CAN DEPEND ON THE LORD!"

Dr. Andrew Bills
Apostle & Founder of Holy Spirit Network Int.
www.hsbn.tv

Made in the USA
Middletown, DE
18 August 2024